WHY HE'S SO LAST MINUTE
—&—
SHE'S GOT IT ALL WRAPPED UP

WHY HE'S SO LAST MINUTE
LAST MINUTE
—&—
SHE'S GOT IT ALL
WRAPPED UP

Allan and Barbara Pease

An Orion paperback
First published in Great Britain in 2007
by Orion Books Ltd
Orion House, 5 Upper St Martin's Lane,
London WC2H 9EA

An Hachette Livre UK company

1 3 5 7 9 10 8 6 4 2

Published by arrangement with Pease International Pty Ltd

Copyright Allan Pease 2007

www.peaseinternational.com

The material in this book has been adapted from *The Definitive
Book of Body Language* copyright © Allan Pease 2004, *Why Men
Don't Listen and Women Can't Read Maps* copyright © Allan Pease
2001 and *Why Men Don't Have A Clue and Women Always Need
More Shoes* copyright © Allan Pease 2002, 2006

A CIP catalogue record for this book
is available from the British Library.

ISBN 978 0 7528 8262 8

Printed and bound in Great Britain by Clays Ltd, St Ives plc

The Orion Publishing Group's policy is to use papers
that are natural, renewable and recyclable products and
made from wood grown in sustainable forests. The logging
and manufacturing processes are expected to conform to
the environmental regulations of the country of origin.

www.orionbooks.co.uk

Contents

Acknowledgements

We would like to thank the following people:

Susan Lamb, Juliet Ewers, Laura Collins, Ian Marshall, Malcolm Edwards, Lisa Milton, Dallas Manderson, Mark Streatfeild and our literary agent, Dorie Simmonds.

INTRODUCTION

Ask anyone – man or woman, old or young – to tell you what they want out of Christmas and they will invariably tell you the same thing: 'I want to spend quality time with the people I love; I want laughter, good food and fun.' It's as simple as that. We all share the same vision. So if men and women want the same thing, why does Christmas so often highlight our differences and divide us rather than bring us closer together? Our good intentions and high hopes for the festive season all too often result in disappointment. Women are left lying in bed at 2 a.m. asking themselves, 'Why are men so bad at buying presents?' and, 'Why don't they pull their weight with the preparations?' Men wake up at 10 a.m. with their partner either no longer talking to them or with a long to-do list and ask themselves, 'Why do women nag so much at Christmas?' and, 'Why do they get so stressed out?' And then there's the question they are *both* asking themselves: 'Why can't we just *enjoy* Christmas?'

In more than three decades of study and research into the differences between men and women, including conducting experiments, analysing reams of film footage, talking on television and giving conferences, we are repeatedly asked one question: 'Why do my partner and I argue so much at Christmas?'

People are genuinely baffled by the kind of things their partner does, and want to know why, at the one time they dedicate to their partner and their family, they seem to argue more than at any other time of year.

Essentially, the answer is simple: because you're different. Put a couple in a room, leave them there for long enough, add some stress in the form of arguing children, possibly a bit too much to drink and most people will argue. Add your mother-in-law and you have a recipe for disaster! The fact is, even in the twenty-first century, the gulf between the sexes is just as wide as it ever was, and at Christmas it can feel like the Grand Canyon.

We spend all year looking forward to Christmas and then all Christmas looking forward to the rest of the year.

Why Christmas Is So Hard on Couples

The divorce rate for newlyweds is now around 50 per cent, and taking defacto and gay relationships into consideration, the real breakup rate for couples is likely to be over 70 per cent. Christmas only adds to our difficulties. Counselling support bodies report that the volume of calls they receive from couples having relationship problems rises significantly during and immediately after the Christmas period. Relate, the UK's largest relationship support group, reports that in some areas of the country, the number of calls to their centres doubles over this period because of the increased demands and pressure placed on couples and families at Christmas.

More than half of people say that they are glad when Christmas is over.

According to recent research, Christmas stress doesn't just affect Christmas week itself – it starts at the beginning of

December, when the good cheer evaporates and is replaced by the realities of planning for the coming month. Greenwich University discovered that from the first Saturday in December, stress increases until the festive period is over.

Concerns about money and debt, unrealistic expectations, packed shopping centres, difficult relatives, caring for children and trying to split time between both partners' families can turn the holiday season into an endurance test.

Many banks have a new kind of Christmas club in operation. The new club helps you save money to pay for last year's gifts.

All those cracks that have been papered over during the year are suddenly exposed and many couples are left in trouble. Stress levels rise and even the smallest things start to irritate us – research from the Halifax shows that 14 per cent of people feel stressed by their neighbours' external Christmas-light displays!

According to a recent poll by Zurich Insurance, a third of people actually dread Christmas. Astonishingly, in a survey carried out by Lloyds TSB, one in 20 people said that they found Christmas harder to cope with and more stressful than divorce or burglary. And according to research, more people apply for divorce in the UK on the first Monday after the New Year – 'Black Monday' – than at any other time of year.

Jim asked his wife, Christine, what she wanted for Christmas. They'd been together for 30 years and he wanted to buy her something special.

'I want to get you something that you'll remember this year. Would you like a new leather coat?' he asked.

'Not really,' said Christine.

'Well, how about a new Mercedes sports car?' said Jim.

'No,' she responded.

'What about a holiday home abroad?' he suggested.

She again rejected his offer.
'Well, what would you like for Christmas?' Jim asked.
'Jim, I'd like a divorce,' answered Christine.
'Sorry, I wasn't planning on spending that much,' said Jim.

Essentially, Christmas is so hard on relationships because it highlights our differences more than any other time of year. If a couple can't communicate and understand each other under pressure – something there is plenty of at Christmas – they are going to find it incredibly difficult to have the happy, harmonious festive season that they both dream of.

A hundred per cent of divorces begin with marriage.
And a lot of them end with Christmas.

It doesn't have to be like this. Christmas can bring you closer together. But in order to communicate effectively, we have to learn to speak the same language. Men and women are different. Not better or worse – different. Just about the only thing they have in common is that they belong to the same species. They live in different worlds, with different values and according to quite different sets of rules. Everyone knows this, but very few people, particularly men, are willing to admit it. If we want to understand each other, we need to learn a new set of rules.

Are Men and Women *Really* Different?

Yes! Men and women have evolved differently because they had to. Women evolved as child-bearers and nest-defenders, and, as a result, female brains became hardwired to nurture, nourish, love and care for the people in their lives. Men evolved with a completely different job description – they were hunters, chasers, protectors, providers and problem-solvers.

As their bodies physically changed to adapt to their specific functions, so did their minds. Men grew taller and stronger than most women, while their brains developed to suit their tasks. Women were mostly content for men to work away as they kept the cave fires burning, and their brains evolved to cope with their function in life.

Over millions of years the brain structures of men and women thus continued to change in different ways. Now, we know the sexes process information differently. They think differently. They believe different things. They have different perceptions, priorities and behaviours. Scientific research, especially the new high-tech brain scans, confirms this. To pretend otherwise is a recipe for heartache, confusion and disillusionment all your life.

The way our brains are wired and the hormones pulsing through our bodies are the two factors that largely dictate, long before we are born, how we will think and behave. Our instincts are simply our genes determining how our bodies will behave in given sets of circumstances.

Women write most of the books on human relations, and over 80 per cent of the purchasers are female. To a neutral observer, this may give the impression that women care more about relationships than men.

In many ways, this is right. The concept of focusing on a relationship is not a natural part of the male psyche, thinking or scale of priorities. But the truth is that men want good, healthy, fulfilling relationships just as much as women. They simply assume that one day a perfect relationship will come along, without the need for prior study or preparation. Women regularly make the mistake of assuming that just because a man loves her, he must also understand her. But he usually doesn't. We call each other the 'opposite' sex for a good reason – we are opposite.

*'A woman needs to know but one man well to
understand all men; whereas a man may know
all women and not understand one of them.'*
HELEN ROWLAND

Why We Wrote This Book

Christmas is all about relationships with loved ones. The secret to a successful Christmas therefore is in understanding one another and learning to work well together in spite of our differences.

There are literally hundreds, if not thousands of books on the market telling you how to have the 'perfect' Christmas – how to bake a Christmas cake, how to decorate your house, how to plan the perfect Christmas dinner with all the trimmings, how to wrap presents, how to make your own Christmas cards and even how to knit the perfect Christmas stocking! – but remarkably there is precious little on the market that will teach you how to have successful and harmonious relationships with your partner and family at Christmas. This is why we wrote *Why He's So Last Minute & She's Got It All Wrapped Up.*

This book offers a real chance to tackle some of the issues that make Christmas so challenging for couples. It's full of common sense and scientific facts that are immensely powerful, yet always presented in a humorous, easily digestible way. It explains the behaviour of the 'other side', whether it happens to be your partner, son, daughter, mother, father, in-laws, friends or neighbours.

Relationships fail because men don't understand why a woman can't be more like a man, and women expect their men to behave just like they do. In this book, we will teach you the key differences between men and women and help you understand why these cause particular conflict at Christmas:

'Why does he hate Christmas shopping?', 'Why does he constantly flick channels when I'm trying to watch a film?', 'Why can't I get on with his mother?' and 'Why does he spend hours playing those little maze puzzles that you get in Christmas crackers?'; 'Why does she cry when she's under pressure?', 'Why does she never like the presents I buy her?' and 'Why can she never put the Christmas tree up straight?' Science can explain all this. We now know that there are evolutional and biological reasons why men and women behave the way they do. Using our research, experience, the most up-to-date studies and surveys, and drawing on everything we have taught in our three previous bestsellers, *The Definitive Guide to Body Language*, *Why Men Don't Listen & Women Can't Read Maps* and *Why Men Don't Have a Clue & Women Always Need More Shoes*, we will offer workable solutions and constructive approaches to understanding your partner and sharing the kind of Christmas you both deserve. But our aim is not simply to make Christmas more enjoyable; we want to make your relationship stronger and more successful for the years to come.

This book is dedicated to all the men and women who have ever sat up in the wee small hours pulling out their hair as they plead with their partners, 'But why don't you understand?' It is for anyone who has ever thought, 'Thank God Christmas only comes once a year.' It is a guidebook to visit a foreign culture or country. It contains local slang and phrases, body language signals and an insight into why the inhabitants are the way they are.

'The best thing about Christmas is that it only comes once a year.'

Why He's So Last Minute & She's Got It All Wrapped Up will help you come to grips with the opposite sex and enjoy Christmas in the way you both want to. Most importantly, it will help you understand yourself and show you how you can both lead happier, healthier and more harmonious lives as a result.

We hope you enjoy our book and have a very happy Christmas!

Barbara and Allan Pease

CHAPTER 1

CHRISTMAS SHOPPING: SURVIVAL OF THE FITTEST

Father Christmas slipping down the chimney to deliver presents is one of the most universal images of Christmas. But how sure are we that he's a man? What if Santa is actually a woman? For starters, Santa does all the shopping in advance – if he were a man, he'd leave it until Christmas Eve and everyone in the world would wake up on Christmas morning to a yapping electronic dog under the tree, still in the bag. Another problem for a male Santa would be delivering all those presents. First of all, even with the reindeer to help him, he'd inevitably get lost and then refuse to stop and ask for directions. Add to this the fact that there would be unavoidable delays in the chimney, where Santa would stop to inspect and repoint bricks in the flue. He would also need to get under every Christmas tree that is crooked to straighten it to a perfectly upright 90-degree angle.

Then again, maybe Santa is a man: after all, he turns up late, eats and then leaves you to do the washing-up. Besides, no woman is going to wear the same outfit, year after year.

How do you know when the shops are about to shut on Christmas Eve? Because your husband is just popping out to start his Christmas shopping.

When it comes to presents and Christmas shopping, men and women have very different ideas and approaches. Shopping is stressful enough at the best of times, but when you're Christmas shopping, it can sometimes feel like an endurance test. Add to that the fact that you have to buy *each other* a present and shopping often becomes a source of arguments and friction. Having said that, nothing is insoluble. It's all a question of good *man*-agement.

Why Men Leave Shopping to the Last Minute and Why They Make Such a Fuss

The great thing about being a man is that you can buy Christmas presents for the entire family in less than 40 minutes at 4.30 p.m. on 24 December and you can do it completely alone. Unfortunately, shopping is almost always man's least favourite occupation. That's part of the reason why he leaves it to the very last minute (or, better still, gets his partner to do it for him). It's also why when he goes clothes shopping, he buys enough to last him for the next nine years.

Most men rate Christmas shopping on a par with having a prostate examination by a doctor with cold hands. British psychologist Dr David Lewis found the stress men experience while Christmas shopping ranks with the kind of stress experienced by a police officer dealing with an angry mob in a riot. For most women, on the other hand, shopping – even Christmas shopping – is a much-loved form of stress relief, provided they have enough time to do it.

Twenty per cent of women have started their Christmas shopping by the beginning of September.

The reasons are obvious for anyone who has studied the different ways men and women evolved, and who understands how their brains are wired. Men's earlier lives as hunters have given them a form of tunnel vision, which enables them to move directly from point A to point B in a straight path. The amount of zigzagging through shoppers and stores needed for a successful Christmas-shopping expedition makes men feel extremely uneasy, as a change of direction requires a more conscious decision. Women, with their wider peripheral vision, however, navigate a crowded shopping centre and zigzag with ease. It doesn't help matters that men leave Christmas shopping to the last minute, when the shops are crammed with more stressed people than a commuter train at rush-hour, but then why do today what you can put off till tomorrow?

....

*'A Christmas shopper's
complaint is one of long-standing.'*
ANON.

....

Men evolved into creatures that made a quick kill and then went home again. Today, that's exactly how men like to shop. They know who they have to buy presents for, they probably have a vague idea of what to get, and they go out and buy all the presents in one go. No agonising over whether Auntie Gladys will like that scarf or this handbag, no deliberating over how much to spend on little James. They go out and buy and then they come home. If they possibly can, they get the presents wrapped at the store. Problem solved.

Women shop the same way as their ancient ancestors would gather food: heading off for the day with a group of other women to a place where someone remembered some tasty things were seen growing. Women tend to start Christmas shopping much earlier than men – and it's not uncommon for some women to start next year's shopping in this year's Christmas sales.

*If a woman is doing her Christmas shopping
in the January sales, she's doing it early.
If a man is doing his Christmas shopping in
the January sales, it's because he's lost and
won't ask directions.*

Often women don't know exactly what they are looking for when doing Christmas shopping, or even which people they are going to buy presents for. As long as they know they have plenty of time ahead, they are happy to spend the day wandering from place to place with a friend in an unstructured way, squeezing, smelling, feeling and tasting all the interesting things they can find, while at the same time talking with each other on a range of unrelated topics. This is because historically women would go out in groups to gather and pick fruit. If nothing was available or ready for picking and they returned home at the end of the day with little to show for their efforts, then so be it. That's why women still feel excited that they have had a great day when they come home from shopping without having bought anything.

'We always hold hands. If I let go, she shops.'
ALLAN PEASE

For men, this is an inconceivable concept. For a man to go out for the day with a group of other men with no clear destination, no clear goals, objectives or time limits and to return home empty-handed would class him as a failure. To men, doing all your Christmas shopping at the last minute in one go is resourceful. There simply isn't time to deliberate – he has to buy 25 Christmas presents in the next hour, so he gets what's available in the time available and leaves.

*Most men get a brain haemorrhage
after 20 minutes of shopping.*

Research shows that not only do men dislike shopping, particularly Christmas shopping, it's detrimental to their health because of the stress it causes them.

Why Women Get So Stressed About Christmas Shopping

As much as women enjoy shopping when they have plenty of time, they are prone to get very anxious and frazzled when they are on a strict timetable, and never is this more the case than at Christmas, particularly as they often shoulder the main responsibility for Christmas shopping. Women can find shopping just as stressful as men.

More than 30 per cent of people find Christmas shopping 'traumatic', compared with 25 per cent who fear the dentist's chair, and 85 per cent of shoppers show serious symptoms of stress while shopping.

Research has revealed that people get particularly stressed when they feel that things are out of control. If a woman has a short amount of time to do her Christmas shopping and she can't find a suitable present, it's understandable that she will become tense and anxious. Added to this, women often have very high expectations of Christmas. They want everything to run smoothly and often think that everyone else's happiness is down to them. It isn't. The advice below should help to take some of the stress out of shopping for both of you.

How to Shop for Presents

If you decide to go present shopping together, you're going to need our help! A recent survey revealed that an astounding 57 per cent of us admit to arguing with our partner while out Christmas shopping. When men and women – with all their differences – go Christmas shopping, the outcome can be explosive. Men become anxious and frustrated when a woman deliberates over exactly what to buy and how much the intended recipient will like something. He just wants her to buy the damn thing so they can get the hell out of there. He gets angry when she asks for his opinion and then buys nothing. In turn, she gets frustrated when he doesn't venture an opinion on her options. She feels she is doing all the work and he's just trailing around after her asking how much longer she's going to be.

Women love considering a wide range of options because it fits the pattern of their brain – a range of emotions and feelings and each different present will reflect that mood. A man's approach to choosing presents reflects the male brain-set – conservative and bottom-line oriented. He tends to choose practical, predictable presents – a bottle of wine, a bouquet of flowers, cufflinks, possibly a scarf or a pair of gloves. Women prefer to give more personal presents that will suit the individual. They want to give the *perfect* present.

To motivate a man to go shopping, give him clear criteria – tell him who he's going to shop for, what you want him to get (colours, sizes, brands, styles) and tell him where you will shop and for how long. With clear objectives (even if you've invented them), you'll be amazed at a man's enthusiasm for shopping.

Writing a list can really help, and shopping online is often a simple and practical solution to getting your Christmas shopping done without the stress.

How to Shop for Clothes as Presents

Often, men and women will buy clothes as Christmas presents. This is another potential source of conflict. To many women, it seems as if men are hardwired to like ugly clothes and this is not far from the truth. For at least a hundred thousand years, women dressed to attract, while men dressed to frighten away their enemies. Men would paint their faces and bodies, put bones through their noses, wear a dead buffalo on their head and have a rock connected to the end of their penis. We should not be surprised if scientists discover men, particularly heterosexual men, have a 'bad taste' clothes gene.

If you want to give a man clothes as a Christmas present and you're asking him to pick out something for himself, or you want him to buy clothes as a gift for another man, give him sizes, colours, fabrics and price ranges, and send him on the hunt. The male brain is organised to concentrate on a singular task. A key to how men shop was revealed in a study with chickens. When chickens were fed male hormones, they pecked at their coloured food in different ways. They ate all the red seed first until it was gone, then all the yellow. The other chickens (with no male hormones) ate all the different coloured food in no order. Most men own two pairs of shoes, male brains have limited skill to match patterns and designs, and one in eight men is colour blind to either red, blue or green.

'When you stop believing in Santa Claus is when you start getting clothes for Christmas.'

If a male partner is buying clothes as a Christmas gift for a woman, she must give him the exact size of the garment she wants. If he gets one size too big, she accuses him of saying she's fat. If it's one size too small, she thinks she's putting on weight. If she is modelling outfits for a man, she only needs to instruct him to rate each outfit from one to ten and should never ask comparison questions like 'Is the green better than the yellow?' If a woman leaves a man waiting outside the changing room in the 'Bored-Husband Seat', she must always get him something to eat.

How to Shop for Food

Food shopping is particularly stressful at Christmas because you have no option but to do it at the last minute and you know you have to get everything you need today because the shops will be closed over the holiday. The problem is, everyone else knows this too and so the shops are crammed with people (and their screaming toddlers, baby buggies and entire family). Here are some tips that should help.

When doing the Christmas food shop, always let a male push the shopping trolley. Men like to be in control and they like to 'drive' it and to use their spatial ability – cornering, angles, speeds and so on. Men even like the trolley with the dummy wheel because that represents an even bigger challenge to their spatial and directional skills. Many men quietly make a *Brrrrrmmmmmm* sound in their heads just like when they were boys.

Ask him how he thinks the food will best fit in the trolley – this lets him use his spatial skills again to get the right answer. Women prefer to zigzag when they shop in a supermarket and work from a list, but men prefer to take a straight line, shop by memory and examine every item that looks good. While you zigzag the aisles, give him clear goals – brands, flavours and sizes – and challenge him to find the best prices and congratulate him when he gets a result. Ask him what he would like to eat over Christmas (if he knows he will be eating his favourite foods, he will be more likely to find them), give him lots of positive strokes and buy him a special treat such as chocolate. A woman may be sticking her fingers down her throat at this point and saying, 'All this just to go food shopping?!' But remember, shopping is not hardwired into the male brain so incentives are needed.

Whatever you do, don't ask a man to do the Christmas food shop without a list – you never know what he'll come back with. Because man evolved as a hunter, he is used to having a defined objective – he knows he has to return with *something*. This is why when a man is asked to buy milk, bread and eggs on the way home from work, he may come home with sardines and marshmallows. He forgot what she asked him to get and came home with a couple of 'bargains' instead – his very own quick kill.

If all else fails, a woman should write her partner a list and ask him to shop online from one of the supermarkets who will deliver to your door. It gives him a practical objective, a timetable and a target to hit – all of which appeal to the way his brain is wired – and will take the stress off both of you.

❄

Even with these strategies, most men still only have a shopping attention span of about 30 minutes. For Christmas shopping, it's probably only 20 minutes. If you insist on taking him Christmas shopping, do it near a large hardware store so that, at worst, he can return home having road-tested the latest Black & Decker double electric reverse router saw which would let him drill perfectly round tiny holes upside down in a plaster ceiling without a ladder, should the need ever arise.

Budgeting for Christmas

Arguing about money and overspending is one of the biggest causes of disputes between couples – particularly over Christmas and in the New Year.

*'About all you can do is dream of a white Christmas,
for it seems like it always leaves most of us in the red.'*

If you are inviting people to you, research shows that you are more likely to spend more money if the receiver is opening their present in front of you. Don't be tempted to spend more than you can afford. This applies in particular to men, as research has shown that men spend more on Christmas presents than women.

The grant-giving charity the Family Welfare Association published a report in 2002 called 'Banishing Scrooge: the Cost of Christmas' that revealed that a family on an average income spent £564 on food, drink, decorations and so forth on Christmas Day alone. Astonishingly, that figure didn't include presents.

*Curb your spending if you want the
festive cheer to last into the New Year.*

According to research by Somerfield, the average spend per person on food at Christmas is £142. Add another £85 on alcohol and it might be cheaper to eat out at Christmas.

*'Oh, for the good old days when people would stop
Christmas shopping when they ran out of money.'*

The best and only solution to make sure that you don't have money worries to contend with in January is to stick to a budget. Do this for food as well as presents.

'Christmas is the time when kids tell Santa what they want and adults pay for it. Deficits are when adults tell the government what they want and their kids pay for it.'

RICHARD LAMM

Why Are Men So Bad at Wrapping Presents?

Most men see wrapping presents as a fruitless exercise. A present is a present whether it's tied up with a bow or not. To them, it is pointless covering something in paper when you're just going to rip it off. A woman likes to see that the giver has taken care and attention in wrapping her gift. To her mind, it is a display of love and affection to see that a present has been wrapped thoughtfully.

Anyone who believes that men are the equal of women has never seen a man trying to wrap a Christmas present.

But there is a scientific reason why men don't like wrapping presents. Men and women's eyes are constructed differently. Men suffer greater eyestrain than women because their eyes are configured for long distances and must be constantly readjusted to look at something close up, such as wrapping a present or reading a newspaper. A woman's eyes are better suited for close-range activities, giving her a longer working time on fine detail. In addition, her brain is wired for coordinated fine-motor capability in a small area. For nest-defending women, being dextrous with both hands would have been an advantage to the process of gathering as it gives twice the speed, so women have evolved to be more dextrous and more likely to be ambidextrous than men, which means the average woman is excellent at tying bows and wrapping fiddly presents.

What's more, women's eyes are better at putting colours together than men's, so when it comes to choosing ribbons that will complement wrapping paper, women's retinas have the advantage. The retina, at the back of the eyeball, contains about 130 million rod-shaped cells called photoreceptors to deal with black and white, and 7 million cone-shaped cells to handle colour. The X chromosome provides these colour cells. Women have two X chromosomes, which gives them a greater variety of cones than men, and this difference is noticeable in how women describe colours in greater detail. A man will use basic colour descriptions like red, blue and green, but a woman will talk of bone, aqua, teal, mauve and apple green.

Besides, there is no mention of the Three Wise Men wrapping the very first Christmas gifts before presenting them to baby Jesus. If there had been wrapping paper, the New Testament would have said something along the lines of: 'And, lo, the gifts were artistically wrapped with paper. And the paper was adorned with pictures of Rudolph the Red-Nosed Reindeer and decorated with curly, glittery ribbon. And Joseph was going to throweth the ribbon away, but Mary saideth unto him, "Keepeth it! That is nice ribbon! Saveth it for next year!" And Joseph did rolleth his eyeballs. And the baby Jesus was more interested in the paper than the frankincense.'

....

How do you know which of your Christmas presents
is from your husband?
Because it's shaped like a power drill and is still in the bag.

....

Why Are Grown Men So Interested in 'Boys' Toys'?

One Christmas we gave a friend of ours, Gerry, a motorised paper stapler that was the size of a miniature television set. It had a see-through plastic case so you could watch all the wheels and dials moving inside. It looked like something out of the Space Shuttle. It took three AA batteries that needed replacing every week and yet all it did was put a staple into a piece of paper – just like any other stapler. Gerry, however, was overjoyed when we gave him this gizmo, not because it was a stapler, but because it had lots of wheels and dials that went round and round, was lit up by flashing lights and made real motor sounds. Gerry told us that sometimes when he gets up in the early hours of the morning to go to the bathroom downstairs, he passes the stapler sitting on the table and can't resist putting four or five staples into a sheet of paper just so he can watch the wheels whizz round.

When his male friends visit him, they all stand around and take turns at putting staples into paper, laughing with delight. Any woman who visits doesn't give it a second glance. They're amazed that anyone could become so excited about such an overpriced piece of equipment that performs the most menial task in the home. But this male behaviour is the equivalent of a woman paying an inflated price for a cuddly teddy bear with oversized eyes and a small nose that was made in Brazil because she 'just couldn't resist it'. If we'd given a woman the stapler for Christmas, she would not have thanked us.

It's easy to explain why the sexes react so differently to such things. Scans of men and women's brains have revealed that men use much more of their brain than women for spatial ability. The spatial part of the brain is the area used for estimating speeds, angles, operating mechanical things and distances – it's the hunting brain.

Because of the spatial arrangement of the male brain, men and boys become addicted to anything that has buttons, a motor or moving parts, makes sounds and has flashing lights. This makes buying presents for men fairly straightforward. Their brains are quite literally wired to enjoy a gift that has these characteristics. This includes any type of video game or computer software, hand-held GPS navigation units, digital cameras, complicated gadgets, lights that go off or on by voice command, anything that has an engine, robotic dogs that act like real dogs and anything that comes with a remote control. If washing machines came with a remote control, men would probably even consider doing the laundry. If it beeps, blinks and needs at least six D-cell batteries, most men want one.

This also explains why men are so interested in DIY gadgets. Even men who have never made anything in their life are drawn to the idea of building things. The entire DIY business is aimed at the spatial area of the male brain. Men love the challenge of assembling classic sailing ships, toy train sets, model aircraft, Meccano sets, computer tables, bookcases or anything that has a set of instructions, however indecipherable they may be.

....

While working as a shopping-centre Father Christmas, I had many children ask for electric trains. 'If you get a train,' I would tell each one, 'you know your dad is going to want to play with it too. Is that OK?'

The usual answer was a quick 'Yes', but after I asked one boy this question, he became very quiet. Trying to move the conversation along, I asked what else he would like Father Christmas to bring him.

He promptly replied, 'Another train.'

....

Essentially, men and boys like similar things. Boys go to toy stores. Men go to DIY stores, hardware shops and car yards where they can find things to make or build or watch work, and thereby satisfy their spatial urges. Boys instinctively believe that as soon as they sprout hair on their chins they will wake up next morning able to completely strip down a car engine and put it all back together.

....

The only difference between men and boys is the price of their toys.

....

Most new business start-ups are now initiated by women, but 99 per cent of all patents – of 'boys' toys' that is – are still registered by men. There's a lesson in this: always buy a man a spatially related toy as a Christmas present. Never give him flowers, a nice card or something decorative for the home; they won't mean a thing to him. Having said that, we also advise you to give him his present toward the end of the day unless you're happy to do all the Christmas chores on your own.

Why Men Buy Foot Spas as Presents

To men, present-giving is another opportunity to help solve problems and give solutions. That's why functional, 'useful' gifts like foot spas, kitchen appliances and so on are so commonly given as gifts to women by men. To appreciate why a man insists on giving solutions to every little thing, there are several things that need to be understood about the way the male brain works.

As we have already seen, men evolved as hunters, and their main contribution to the survival of the human race was the ability to hit a moving target so everyone could eat. They needed to be able to aim accurately at either edible targets or enemies who either wanted to steal that food or who threatened their families. As a result, their brains evolved with a target-hitting area called the 'visual-spatial' area that allows them successfully to carry out their whole reason for being: hitting targets and solving problems. They turned into results-oriented people who measure their own success by results, accomplishments and their ability to come up with solutions to problems. As a consequence, a man still defines who he is and his self-worth by his problem-solving abilities and achievements. Therefore men buy women something that they think will solve a problem and be useful in some way.

> *'At Christmas, we always exchange presents.*
> *I exchange the one she gives me, she exchanges*
> *the one I give her.'*

Presents not to buy your female partner for Christmas include any kind of household appliance or something that is going to make 'housework easier' – for instance, a blender, a toaster, a new vacuum-cleaner, one of those mops they advertise on TV that does everything but suck the life out of you and anything in a bigger dress size than she is.

> *Ben was in the department store looking for a Christmas gift for his wife.*
> *'How about some perfume?' he said to the cosmetics sales assistant. She showed him a bottle costing £30.*
> *'That's a bit much,' said Ben, so she returned with a smaller bottle for £15.*
> *'That's still quite a bit,' Ben complained.*
> *Growing disgusted, the sales assistant brought out a tiny £5 bottle.*
> *Ben grew agitated: 'What I mean,' he said, 'is I'd like to see something really cheap.'*
> *So the sales assistant handed him a mirror.*

Case Study: Helen and Andy

Helen and Andy are opening their Christmas presents. Helen has done all the present shopping except for her own present from Andy and she can't wait to see what he has bought her. Andy was thrilled with his new GPS system for his car. It was exactly what he wanted and he can't wait to try it out. He reaches under the Christmas tree and, beaming, passes Helen a large gift-wrapped box. 'Happy Christmas,' he says.

Helen has been eyeing the present under the tree for days. She has been dropping hints about an Italian leather handbag she saw in the department store for some time. She has deliberately lingered when walking past it for several weeks now and has showed Andy a picture of it in a magazine. She hasn't told him explicitly that she wants it for Christmas, because she still wants him to put some thought into it and she likes her present to be a surprise, but she is hopeful that he has understood what she wants. She rips open the wrapping paper, hardly able to contain her excitement.

HELEN: (her face falling) 'You bought me a blender?'
ANDY: (proudly) 'No, not just any blender: it's a *very good* blender. It's top of the range. The man in the store says it's got fifteen different settings and has been given a five-star rating by *Which?* magazine . . . Is it not the one you wanted?'
HELEN: 'It's not that . . . It's just . . . '
ANDY: 'You're always saying how the one you've got isn't very good.'
HELEN: 'I know, it's just . . . well . . . I guess I wanted you to get me something that showed you cared, that you'd thought about me.'
ANDY: 'I do care. I did think about you – I thought you needed a blender. What did you want?'
HELEN: (close to tears) 'I wanted a handbag.'
ANDY: (completely at a loss) 'Well, how was I supposed to know that? I'm not a mind-reader. You said you needed a new blender the other day.'
HELEN: (storming out of the room) 'You don't understand me at all!'

This is a common problem at Christmas. Andy's approach to buying a present is to buy something useful. He genuinely thinks he is being caring and loving by trying to solve a problem for Helen. She always says that he doesn't listen to her, but he listened to her need for a new blender and has given her a thoughtful surprise. She thinks he doesn't understand her emotional needs.

'It's the thought that counts.'
'What the hell were you thinking?'

A woman wants a man to buy her an 'emotional' present, something personal, possibly something romantic. It's not that men don't want to romance women, it's just that they don't understand its importance to women. Women spend millions every year on romantic novels. Women's magazines concentrate on love, romance, other people's affairs or how to exercise, eat and dress better to have even more romance. Conversely, men spend millions on books and magazines teaching technical know-how on a range of spatially related subjects, from computers and mechanical apparatus to lunch-chasing activities like fishing, hunting and football.

A recent survey found that jewellery is desired as a Christmas gift by 65 per cent of women, but only 42 per cent of men will give it as a present. Nearly 40 per cent of women would love to be whisked away on holiday as a Christmas present, but only 7 per cent of men have considered this.

It's no wonder when it comes to romantic presents that most men generally don't know what to do. This is understandable, as a modern man has never had a role model. His father didn't know what to do either, as it was never an issue for him. A woman at one of our conferences recently said that she had asked her husband to show her more affection – so he washed and polished her car. This demonstrates how men see 'doing things' as a way of showing they care. The same husband bought her a car jack for Christmas and got her front-row seats at a wrestling match for their tenth wedding anniversary.

What a woman wants for Christmas is something that shows her that her partner understands her, knows what she likes and that shows how he feels about her.

....

A guy bought his wife a beautiful diamond ring for Christmas. After hearing about this extravagant gift, a friend of his said, 'I thought she wanted one of those sporty four-wheel-drive vehicles.'

'She did,' he replied. 'But where was I going to find a fake Jeep?'

....

Advice for Men – Why Shoes Are the Ultimate Gift

If a man is serious about buying his female partner a gift she'll love this Christmas, maybe he should consider buying her shoes . . . Shoes aren't something most men would think of giving as a present, but research shows that whether it is moccasins or sandals, women everywhere are shoe-obsessed. On average, female Inuit (Eskimos) own four pairs of snow-shoes to every one pair that their male counterpart owns. In the Philippines, studies revealed that women own 12 pairs of shoes to every pair owned by men.

....

'They went into my closets looking for skeletons, but thank God all they found were shoes, beautiful shoes.'

IMELDA MARCOS

....

Unlike clothes, which are often disappointing for women because most things won't fit, they look bad or highlight a woman's liabilities, shoes don't fit into these categories because women don't have to diet to fit into them. In order to buy shoes for a woman, all you have to know is her size. And they never make your bum look big . . .

Beautiful shoes distract from trouble spots on the rest of a woman's body. Unlike clothes, shoes don't care if a woman has missed the last six sessions at the gym, overindulged on Christmas pudding or has a stomach bulge. Shoes never make a woman feel that she's not thin enough, and in fact, in the right high-heeled shoes, a woman's weight is distributed over a greater height!

Shoes might be sorted into colour or style categories, but women need never split their wardrobe into fat, skinny or normal shoes. Unless she's pregnant, the rule is, once a shoe size, always a shoe size – feet don't bloat from a size 6 to size 9 because of eating too many After Eight or roast potatoes.

Feet never betray a woman because, basically, they are one part of the body that doesn't go up and down in weight, so when women are feeling a little thick in the waist, shoes are the solution! There is no guilt associated with trying on shoes, and women never have to be embarrassed about their shoe size.

Women are as obsessed with shoes as men are with sports and spatial toys, so don't fight or criticise it; instead, use this knowledge to your advantage. If you want to be a big hit with a woman this Christmas, take her shoe shopping and make a secret note of the brands, size and colours of the shoes she loves, then secretly return to the store, purchase them and give them to her to make her Christmas Day extra special.

Buying a woman shoes for Christmas can have other benefits, too. Unlike other forms of envy, shoe envy is a very public condition. While Cinderella's ugly sisters epitomised the nastier side of this female quirk, shoe envy is part of the female sisterhood. Women unashamedly point, stare and comment on a great pair of shoes. It's a healthy and normal part of the female psyche. That means that once her friends hear that you bought her shoes for Christmas, you'll not only become the girl-talk of the town, your love life will dramatically improve.

And the absolute worst present you could give your partner for Christmas? It has to be a diet book . . . According to a survey by MSN Shopping, 7 per cent of men who responded have committed the ultimate gift gaffe and bought their partner a diet book or exercise video as a very unsubtle festive 'hint'.

Buying Christmas Presents for Children

As a little girl climbed on to Santa's lap, Santa asked the usual 'And what would you like for Christmas?'

The child stared at him open-mouthed and horrified, then gasped, 'Didn't you get my email?'

We all want our children to have a wonderful time at Christmas, but sometimes they can put a lot of pressure on us to spend more than we'd like to on their presents – whether it's a new pair of trainers, a skateboard or a Wendy house. Part of this is the effect of the increasing commercialisation of Christmas, but it has to be said that children are also the absolute masters of the art of manipulation.

'From a commercial point of view, if Christmas did not exist it would be necessary to invent it.'
KATHERINE WHITEHORN

Up to this point, we have focused on the humorous aspects of relationships, but you should be aware that if your child puts pressure on you to buy a certain present and continues to pressurise you even though you have said that it is not possible and starts to make threats, then essentially you are being emotionally blackmailed. Most people never consider that those close to them, least of all a child, could use this type of manipulative strategy; they just think that the child is being 'persistent' and is responding to adverts and peer pressure. Children learn early that emotional blackmail is a way of getting what they want – particularly when they know their parents use it too. Children feel relatively powerless because of their age and size, so blackmail can look like the easiest and most effective route to getting the Christmas present they're hankering after. This may well be learned behaviour – if you or your partner use manipulation to get your own way, it is likely that your children will follow suit. Parents who routinely try to emotionally blackmail their children must always be ready to have the tables turned on them.

Adults who use emotional blackmail raise children who are even better at it.

Case Study: Anna and Katie

Anna was a single parent and had a very limited budget for Christmas presents. She wanted to buy her daughter, Katie, something special, but really couldn't afford to overspend. Katie had set her heart on a very expensive Barbie house, complete with furniture, garden accessories, sports car and clothing. It was way beyond Anna's means, and as she didn't want Katie to be disappointed on Christmas Day, Anna had to tell her that she would get her a very lovely present but she wouldn't be able to get such a large one. She planned to buy just the house and then to buy the smaller pieces for her birthday and ask friends and relatives to do the same. Katie desperately wanted everything, as her best friend had the whole range. After persisting for a while and receiving the same response from Anna, Katie started to say things like 'All my friends have everything. Their parents must love them more than you love me,' and 'People at school will laugh at me.' Anna started to feel increasingly guilty. She didn't want her daughter not to fit in or to be considered mean. Katie continued to pester Anna and eventually said, 'You don't love me. If Daddy was here, he'd buy it all.' In the end, Anna felt so guilty that she gave in and on Christmas Day Katie got exactly what she wanted. Anna didn't feel any better for giving in to Katie's demands, though.

❋

In this case study, we can see that Katie homed in on Anna's deepest vulnerabilities – that she wasn't a loving parent, that her daughter was suffering because she was a single parent and that her daughter would be ostracised. Other common tactics include:

❋ 'If you really loved me, you'd buy it for me.'
❋ 'I'll run away – I must be adopted.'
❋ 'You love my sister more than me.'
❋ 'I'll cry on Christmas Day and then you'll be sorry.'

In the process of complying, the blackmailer has made you feel bad about yourself, and guilty for resisting.

One day, we were watching a busker on the streets of London. At the end of his act, he turned to the group of spellbound children who were watching him and called out, 'Hey, kids! If your parents won't give you £1 to put in my hat, it means they don't love you!' He raised £18.

The more anyone gives in to emotional blackmail, the more it will become a pattern that dictates the future of a relationship. The closer the relationship, the greater the sense of guilt, and guilt is the most powerful tool of the blackmailer.

Unless you are happy to comply with your child's demands, and to accept the fact that they will become more frequent, the only way to deal with a child who is manipulating you is to stand firm. Have some responses ready. Stand firm and your child will respect you more.

'Really, You Shouldn't Have'

So what happens when somebody gives you a present that you really don't like? That fluffy jumper from your grandma with a Christmas cracker knitted on it? A set of coasters with a hunting scene on them? Part of getting on with your family at Christmas and making them feel special is showing your appreciation for the fact that they have thought about you – even if you wish they hadn't.

In a recent survey, one in 20 people said that their partner never buys them what they want for Christmas.

In general, it's people's body language, not their words that give them away. No matter how convincingly and graciously you say, 'Thank you, I love it!' if your body language is saying something different, you can guarantee that the gift-giver will realise this. The difficulty with lying is that the subconscious mind acts automatically and independently of our verbal lie, so our body language gives us away. This is why people who rarely tell lies are easily caught, regardless of how convincing they may sound. The moment they begin to lie, their body sends out contradictory signals, and these give us a feeling that they're not telling the truth. During the lie, the subconscious mind sends out nervous energy, which appears as a gesture that can contradict what was said.

It's obvious, then, that to be able to lie successfully, you need to have your body hidden or out of sight. Lying is easier if you're sitting where your body is partially hidden, peering over a fence or from behind a closed door. The best way to lie is over the telephone or in a letter. If it's possible, therefore, send a thank-you letter to the person who has given you the present. That way, there really isn't much chance that they'll know how much you don't like it.

If they give the present to you directly and are there when you open it, this isn't an option. One solution is to simply say 'thank you' as sincerely as you can and give the person a hug. That way, you don't have to lie directly. If they question you further – 'Are you sure you like it? Is it your style?' – your best bet is probably just to tell the truth as tactfully and kindly as you can. It is very difficult to lie effectively, even about something small.

It may be that you have given somebody a present and you really aren't sure whether they like it or hate it. When lying, most people make one of seven common mistakes, so if you want to find out whether your present will be doing the rounds of the charity shops come the New Year, look out for one or more of the following:

1 The Mouth Cover

The hand covers the mouth as the brain subconsciously instructs it to try to suppress the deceitful words that are being said. Sometimes this gesture might only be several fingers over the mouth or even a closed fist, but its meaning remains the same.

2 The Nose Touch

Sometimes the Nose Touch can be several quick rubs below the nose or it may be one quick, almost imperceptible touch. Women perform this gesture with smaller strokes than men, perhaps to avoid smudging their make-up.

American neurologist Alan Hirsch and psychiatrist Charles

Wolf did an extensive analysis of Bill Clinton's testimony to the Grand Jury on his affair with Monica Lewinsky and found that, when he told the truth, he rarely touched his nose. When he lied, however, he gave a split-second frown before he answered and touched his nose once every four minutes for a grand total of 26 Nose Touches.

3 The Eye Rub

When a child doesn't want to look at something he'll cover his eyes with one or both hands. When an adult doesn't want to look at something distasteful – such as that horrendous pink mohair jumper – the Eye Rub is likely to occur. The Eye Rub is the brain's attempt to block out the deceit, doubt or distasteful thing it sees, or to avoid having to look at the face of the person who is being lied to. Men usually rub their eyes vigorously, and if the lie is a real whopper, they will often look away. Women are less likely to use the Eye Rub – instead, they will use small, gentle touching motions just below the eye, because they either have been conditioned as girls to avoid making robust gestures or to avoid smudging make-up. They also avoid a listener's gaze by looking away.

4 The Ear Grab

Imagine you tell someone, 'I hope you like it. It only costs £300,' and the person grabs their ear, looks away to the side and responds, 'It was worth every penny.' This is a symbolic attempt by the listener to 'hear no evil': trying to block the words he is hearing by putting the hand around or over the ear or tugging at the earlobe. This is the adult version of the Hands-Over-Both-Ears gesture used by the child who wants to block out his parent's reprimands. Other variations of the Ear Grab include rubbing the back of the ear, the Finger Drill – where the fingertip is screwed back and forth inside the ear, pulling at the earlobe or bending the entire ear forward to cover the ear hole.

5 The Neck Scratch

The index finger – usually of the writing hand – scratches the side of the neck below the earlobe. Our observations of this gesture reveal the person scratches an average of five times. Rarely is the number of scratches less than five and hardly ever more than five. This gesture is a signal of doubt or uncertainty and is therefore characteristic of the person who isn't sure that they like the gift they have been given. It is very noticeable when the verbal language contradicts it – for example, when the person is saying something positive like 'I love it' but the Neck Scratch indicates they don't.

6 Fingers-in-the-Mouth

This is an unconscious attempt by the person to revert to the security of the child sucking on his mother's breast and occurs when a person feels under pressure. This is a classic response when you don't want to hurt someone's feelings when they've given you a present they've put a lot of thought or effort into. A young child substitutes his thumb or a blanket for his mother's breast and, as an adult, he puts his fingers to his mouth.

7 Concealed Hands

When children are lying or concealing something, they'll often hide their palms behind the back. Similarly, when a man tells you he loves the novelty socks you bought him for Christmas but his hands are in his pockets, or in an arms-crossed position, you will be able to tell that he's not being truthful. A woman who is trying to hide the truth will try to avoid the subject or talk about a range of unrelated topics while doing various other activities at the same time.

Salespeople are taught to watch for a customer's exposed palms when he gives reasons or objections about why he can't buy a product, because when someone is giving valid reasons, they usually show their palms. When people are being open in explaining their reasons, they use their hands and flash their palms, whereas someone who isn't telling the truth is likely to give the same verbal responses but conceal their hands.

Reading Between the Lines of Gift-Giving

When someone says . . .	What they really mean . . .
'I really don't deserve this.'	'What did I do to deserve this?'
'You shouldn't have.'	'I wish you hadn't.'
'Well, well, well . . .'	'Just you wait until next year.'
'What a pity it's not my size.'	'Are you trying to tell me I'm fat?'
'Oh, no, that's a shame – I've got one of these already.'	'And it's much nicer than this.'

Remember that the important thing is not what you give, or how you wrap it. The important thing, during this very special time of year, is to save the receipt.

Chapter 2

MEN, WOMEN AND CHRISTMAS STRESS

A woman was out Christmas shopping with her two children. After many hours of looking at row after row of toys and everything else imaginable, and hearing both her children asking for everything they saw on those many shelves, this woman finally made it out of the store and to the lift with her two kids.

She was feeling what so many of us feel during the Christmas season: overwhelming pressure to go to every party, every housewarming, taste all the festive food and treats, get that perfect gift for every single person on our shopping list, make sure we don't forget anyone on our card list and respond to everyone who sends us a card. Not to mention getting the children everything they ask for.

Finally the lift doors opened – there was already a crowd inside. This woman pushed her way in and dragged her two children in with her, along with all her bags of shopping.

When the doors closed, she let out a big sigh and decided she couldn't take it any more, saying out loud, to no one in particular, 'Whoever started this whole Christmas thing should be strung up!'

From the back of the elevator, a quiet, calm voice responded, 'Don't worry, madam – I believe they crucified him.'

Christmas is an incredible time . . . incredible that we survive it every year. There's the stress of dealing with family, worrying about last-minute shopping, gritting your teeth and laughing at your boss's terrible jokes and coping with overexcited, over-stimulated children. With every door that's opened on the advent calendar, it feels like our blood pressure rises. By the time it's Christmas Eve, most of us are cursing every time we hear 'Last Christmas' by Wham! or Slade's 'Merry Xmas, Everybody' and wishing we'd started planning everything months earlier.

In 2006 trade unions and activists asked the British government to investigate the negative impact of Christmas music on shop workers who continually listen to the songs all day. The music was described as 'torture', the 'forgotten pollutant' and detrimental to their sanity.

The secret to avoiding festive stress is to plan ahead and not take on too much, but this is easier said than done, and even with the best will in the world the run-up to Christmas leaves most of us frazzled and tired.

According to mental-health charity Mind, one in five of us gets stressed during the festive season.

Men and women both agree that Christmas is a busy and stressful time, but in other ways, the differences between the sexes are never more apparent than over the festive period. Women and men need to learn to work together effectively if they want to have the kind of relaxed, stress-free Christmas they both hope for, and the only way they will be able to achieve this is if they each learn to understand their differences and communicate their needs in a way that the other understands. The sexes have different ways of dealing with festive stress and have different responses to it. Our research has shown that the vast majority of problems and disagreements between the sexes are due to fundamental differences in the way our brains function and in the way that we communicate. In this chapter, we will address some of these differences and look at how understanding them can help take the stress out of the festive season.

How Women Deal With Christmas Stress

When a woman is under pressure at Christmas, or at any time of year, her speech function is activated and she starts talking, often non-stop. If she's stressed, she talks, talks and talks to anyone who will listen. She can talk to her mother or her friends about her Christmas worries for hours, giving a thorough report of details. She talks about current problems ('I hope Joan likes her gift; I'm worried I've got the wrong size'), past problems ('I'm not doing what I did last year again – my sister's kids are hard work'), possible problems ('What if I run out of food?') and problems that have no solutions ('What if people don't have a good time?').

It is a fact that women often bear the brunt of Christmas stress – research reveals that women take on more of the responsibility for shopping, cooking and decorating than men (an issue we'll look at in more detail in Chapter 3). Women's reaction to stress is to talk. It is mainly because of their better ability to cope with stress that women live an average of seven years longer than men.

Women talk about their problem over and over, backwards and forwards and from every angle. They don't necessarily want to reach any conclusions. Talking about their problems is how they relieve their stress. When she talks, no solutions are sought, as she receives comfort and relief from the process of talking. Her talk is unstructured, and several subjects can be discussed at any one time with no conclusions being reached.

Women cope with Christmas stress by talking.

Why Women List Out Loud Everything They've Got to Do

'My wife drives me crazy at Christmas,' said a man at one of our seminars. 'She talks out loud about what she's got to do – the options, possibilities, people involved and what we'll be doing, when, where and with whom. She talks about what she wants to buy everyone. Then she talks about whether they'll like their presents and whether she can return things if they don't. She talks about everything! It's so distracting. I can't concentrate on anything!'

A woman will verbalise a series of items out loud in random order, listing all the options and possibilities.

A woman's brain is pre-wired to use speech as a main form of expression and this is one of her strengths. If a man has to carry out a list of five or six tasks, he will say, 'I've got some things to do. I'll see you later.' A woman will verbalise all the items out loud in random order, mentioning all options and possibilities. She will say, 'Let's see, I've got to pick up the turkey, get some more wrapping paper, buy Daniel's present, then I'll pick up the parcel from the post office, ring Jane and ask her what time she'll arrive here on Christmas Day . . .' This is one of the reasons men accuse women of talking too much.

At Christmas, women will often give men a long list of things that they are worried about. They will list aloud everything there is to do and when it has to be done by, including who they need to send cards to, what they think you should cook on Christmas Day, when to do the Christmas shopping, who to invite and not invite and why – talking about it makes them feel better and it makes them better at coping with festive stress.

Why Women Cry When They Get Stressed

There are many reasons why women cry – including to cleanse the eyes and as an emotional device – but it has been proven that crying is a stress-reducer. Chemical analysis of tears reveals that stress tears, those that roll down the cheek, contain different proteins from those used for eye cleansing. The body appears to use this function to clear stress toxins from the body. This could explain why women say they feel better after a 'good cry', even when there appears to be no real reason for crying. Tears also contain endorphins, one of the body's natural painkillers, which act as a damper to emotional pain.

Why Women Get Upset by Men's Solutions to Christmas Catering

Annie doesn't know what to cook on Christmas Day. Her daughter loves goose; her son wants chicken; she wouldn't mind trying something completely different like pheasant; and although everyone likes turkey, they had that last year. She starts telling her husband, Jack, about the problem, but before she's even got halfway through telling him, he interrupts and says, 'Just do turkey – it's traditional and everybody likes it.' Then he leaves the room. Annie is furious. She wants to talk through the options and Jack just wades in with a solution. If she says she's worried about cooking for so many people, he'll say they should eat out on Christmas Day. If she says she doesn't know whether to do cranberry sauce or bread sauce, he'll say both. If she says she finds Christmas stressful, he says next year they'll go away for Christmas. Why does he insist on solving every problem she brings up?

Under stress or pressure, a man's main brain functions of spatial ability and logic are activated. For a man, listening to her talk about problems is hard work because he feels he is expected to solve each problem she brings up as she talks aloud. He doesn't just want to talk about it; he wants to do something about it! He is likely to interrupt with, 'What's the point here?' The point is that there doesn't need to be a point. The most valuable lesson a man can learn is to listen using listening sounds and gestures, and not offer solutions. To a man, however, this is an alien concept because he only talks when he has a solution to offer.

When you're dealing with an upset woman, don't offer solutions or invalidate her feelings – just show her you're listening.

When a woman refuses to accept his solutions, his next strategy is to try to minimise the problems by telling her, 'It doesn't really matter,' 'You're overreacting,' 'Forget about it,' and, 'It's not a big deal.' Or, worst of all, 'Why do you make such a fuss about Christmas every year? It's meant to be *fun*.' This is usually followed by something like 'This happens every year – you invite all these people and take on too much and then you get all stressed out. Next year we're going away for Christmas.' This infuriates a woman, who begins to feel he doesn't care about her because he won't listen.

Talking about her problems is how a woman gets relief from stress at Christmas. But she wants to be heard, not fixed.

Why Men Offer Seasonal Solutions

Men have logical, problem-solving minds. When a man enters a room in a conference centre or restaurant for the first time, he looks around and sees things that need fixing and better ways of laying out the room. His brain is a problem-solving machine that never takes a holiday. Even if he was on his deathbed in hospital he'd be thinking of better ways to arrange the ward to take advantage of the natural light and country views.

If a woman has spent all afternoon putting up Christmas decorations, a man will walk in and straighten the Christmas tree – he looks for a problem to fix.

When a woman talks about her problems, a man continually interrupts her and offers solutions. He can't help himself because his brain is programmed to do this. He thinks she will feel much better when she has a solution. She only wants to talk and ignores his solutions. This makes him feel incompetent and a failure or that she is probably blaming him for her problems. Women don't want solutions; they just want to talk about things and for someone to listen. The best thing a husband can do to help a wife who is stressed at Christmas is listen.

Men need to understand that when a woman is stressed, she wants to talk, and all he needs to do is listen, not offer solutions.

Case Study: Sarah and Paul

Christmas is just round the corner and Sarah has had a tough day at work: she has got a deadline right before Christmas, and the boss now wants her to come in between Christmas and New Year. Her parents are separated and she's worried her dad is upset that she's inviting her mum and not him for Christmas this year. On top of all that, she doesn't know how she's going to find time to do her Christmas shopping. She feels like her world is falling apart and wants to talk to Paul about it when he gets home.

She prepares a good dinner in the expectation that they'll have a long heart-to-heart as they eat. He'll be loving and sympathetic. She'll be able to pour out her heart to someone who cares and she knows she'll feel so much better as a result. She wants him to listen, make her feel loved and understood, and reassure her that she'll be able to solve her problems.

But Paul has also had a tough day. His Christmas bonus this year wasn't very good and he's worrying about how they are going to be able to afford all the luxuries they have planned for the festive season. As he drives home, his mind is working overtime on the solutions. He really needs time out to sort out his own problems.

He arrives home, says a quick 'Hi' to Sarah and then sits down in the lounge to watch the news on television. She checks the meal and tells him dinner will be ready in 15 minutes. He thinks, 'Good! Fifteen minutes of quiet time before we eat.' Sarah thinks, 'Great! Fifteen minutes to start chatting before we eat.'

SARAH: 'How was your day, darling?'

PAUL: 'Fine.'

SARAH: 'Mine was terrible. I just can't take any more!'

PAUL: (still with half an eye on the news) 'You can't take any more of what?'

SARAH: 'My boss is pressuring me about this deadline and now he wants me to come into work on Boxing Day. Then he told me he wanted the deadline met on the 23rd, not Christmas Eve. When I tried to explain that was impossible because I'm still working on the Seinfeld project, he just cut me off and said he didn't want to hear any more excuses. Can you believe it? He just wouldn't listen to me . . . (becoming upset) . . . I just feel like quitting. And as if that weren't enough, I've got all these Christmas presents to buy, my dad is clearly upset with me, and I don't think I can take any more stress . . .'

PAUL: 'Look, it's simple, Sarah . . . what you should do is stand up for yourself and tell your boss you can't finish both projects and ask which he wants completed first. Tell him you've already planned to go away for Christmas and there's no way you can go in on Boxing Day. Tell your dad he can come to us next year, or for New Year's Eve. And buy the presents online at the weekend.'

SARAH: (becoming emotional) 'I can't believe you! I'm telling you about how much pressure I'm under, and then you start telling me what to do. Why can't you just listen to me? I'm sick of men always knowing better.'

PAUL: 'Come on, Sarah. If you don't want my opinion, stop telling me your problems. Sort it out yourself and stop complaining to me about it! I have enough of my own problems, which, by the way, I always sort out myself!'

SARAH: (close to tears) 'Well, you can go jump! I'll find some-one else who'll listen to me and won't tell me what I did wrong! You can get your own dinner! I'm going out and I don't know when I'll be back!'

For men and women around the world, it's an all-too-common scenario. At the end of it, Sarah feels let down, unloved and hurt. Paul feels unappreciated and confused because Sarah has just criticised his number-one skill: problem-solving.

How could Paul have handled it better? Let's rewind this scene and see how Paul could have avoided having such a bad night.

SARAH: 'How was your day, darling?'

PAUL: 'It was fine. I didn't get the bonus I'd hoped for, but I think I can work things out.'

SARAH: 'I've had the worst day of my life and I just can't take any more!'

PAUL: 'Oh, no. You poor darling! I want you to tell me all about it, but can I have fifteen minutes by myself to sort out the money situation, then I'll be able to give you my full attention over dinner.'

SARAH: 'OK . . . I'll call you when it's ready. Would you like a glass of wine now?'

PAUL: 'Thanks, darling . . . I'd love one.'

By Paul asking for time out and Sarah granting it, he now has the time and space to sit on his rock and think about his own problems. Sarah feels reassured and happy that he'll be there for her over dinner, when she'll be able to get her problems off her chest and feel better about life.

Here's how the dinner went:

SARAH: 'My boss is giving me a really hard time. When I got into work this morning, he told me he's brought forward the deadline to the 23rd, which is impossible because I'm still working on the Seinfeld project that he'd told me was urgent . . .'

PAUL: (showing interest with his face) 'Darling . . . that's terrible. Doesn't he know how hard you've been working? You look so stressed . . .'

SARAH: 'You can't begin to imagine how stressed I am! Christmas is a nightmare anyway without him piling on the pressure. So then I started to explain it wasn't completed because the Seinfeld project is so time-consuming. But in the middle of my explanation he just cuts me off and says he doesn't want to hear any excuses! Then he said he needs me at work on Boxing Day. Can you believe it?'

PAUL: (looking concerned and resisting giving advice) 'Sounds like he's really giving you a tough time . . .'

SARAH: 'He just wouldn't listen to me . . . I am so stressed I feel like quitting . . . And then I'm worried about my dad because he's not coming for Christmas, and I haven't even started my Christmas shopping.'

PAUL: (putting his arm round her) 'You've had a really hard time, honey. What would you like to do?'

SARAH: 'I'm going to sleep on it tonight and get up early tomorrow and if I don't feel any better, I'd really like you to help me work out how to handle everything. I'm just too tired and stressed out to discuss it tonight. Thanks for listening to me, darling. I feel so much better . . .'

By not offering immediate solutions, Paul avoided an argument, got a glass of wine and didn't end up sleeping alone on the couch. By giving Paul time to himself, Sarah avoided the usual arguments and felt happy about herself and her life.

Solution: How to Deal With a Woman Who Is Stressed at Christmas

If a woman is upset or stressed about Christmas and needs to talk, a simple technique is to say to a man, 'I need to talk with you about Christmas. I don't need any solutions; I just want you to listen.' A man will be happy with this approach because he knows exactly what he is supposed to do.

If a woman is talking and a man does not know whether she is asking for solutions or just talking, he can find out by simply asking, 'Would you like me to listen as a boy or a girl?' If she wants him to listen as a girl, he only has to listen. If she wants him to listen as a boy, he can offer solutions. Either way, both will be happy because each understands what is expected.

How Men Deal With Christmas Stress

What about when a man is worried about Christmas? It is a common misconception that men love Christmas and women hate it – it is actually men who fret more about Christmas and are less inclined to enjoy it. In an ICM poll in 2004, 80 per cent of women said they love Christmas, compared with only 68 per cent of men. This is probably in large part due to money worries – men spend more on presents at Christmas and are more likely to bear the responsibility for Christmas extravagance.

When a man is stressed about any aspect of Christmas, he is likely to clam up and stop talking. A woman talks outside her head – that is, you can hear her, whereas a man talks inside his head. He doesn't have strong brain areas for speech, so this suits his mindset. When he has a problem, he talks to himself, while she talks to other people.

Silent Night – Why Stressed Men Won't Talk

A man uses his right brain to try to solve his problems or find solutions and he stops using his left brain to listen or speak. His brain can only do 'one thing at a time'. He can't solve problems and listen or talk simultaneously. This silence is often distressing and frightening for a woman. A women says to her husband, son or brother, 'Come on, you've got to talk about it! You'll feel better!' She says this because this is what works for her. But he just wants to be left alone to fire-gaze until he comes up with some solutions and answers.

Men evolved as warriors, protectors and problem-solvers. Their brain bias and social conditioning prevent them from showing fear or uncertainty. Men talk mainly inside their heads because they don't have the verbal capability that women have to use words externally for communication. When a man is sitting staring out of a window, a brain scan shows that he is having a conversation with himself – inside his head.

The famous Rodin sculpture 'The Thinker' symbolises a man thinking about his problems. He wants to sit on his rock and think about solutions and needs to be alone to do it. The key word here is 'alone'.

If Rodin created a sculpture to personify a woman, it would probably be called 'The Talker'. Women need to understand that when a man is on his rock they need to leave him there and let him think. Many women feel that his silence means he doesn't love her or that he's angry with her. This is because if a woman wasn't talking, she'd be angry or upset. But if she leaves him on his rock with a cup of tea and a mince pie and doesn't press him to talk, he'll be fine. When he finally solves his problem, he'll come down off his rock and feel happy and begin to talk again.

When a woman tries to get a man to talk about his feelings or problems, he resists because he sees it as criticism, or feels that she must think he is incompetent and she has a better solution for him. In reality, her objective is to help him feel better, and for a woman, offering advice builds trust in a relationship and is not seen as a sign of weakness.

At Christmas, the different ways men 'sit on their rock' include reading a newspaper or magazine, watching television, playing a computer game, retreating to their workshop or going to the gym. It seems that stimulating his spatial area speeds up the problem-solving process, which is why men like to undertake an activity such as golf when thinking about problems.

Solution: How to Deal with a Man Who Is Stressed at Christmas

A woman needs to understand that a man's fire-gazing is his way of relieving stress, and that she should not take it personally. If you think there is something worrying him, do not offer advice when he didn't ask for it, as it will be seen by him as a statement that she feels he is incompetent because he can't solve his own problems. When he goes quiet at Christmas, it is probably because he is working something out in his head or he just needs time out.

What About When Christmas Stress Is Affecting Them *Both*?

At Christmas, uptight men get drunk. Uptight women hit the Quality Street and the Boxing Day sales. Under pressure, women talk without thinking and men act without thinking. That's why 90 per cent of people in jails are men and 90 per cent of people who see therapists are women. When men and women are both under pressure at Christmas, it can be an emotional minefield as each tries to cope. Men stop talking and women become worried about it. Women start talking and men can't handle it. This partly explains why so many couples apply for divorces in January, when they've spent long periods of time together and have found that their inability to communicate has brought them to the end of the line.

This is one of the least understood stress differences between men and women. A man will completely shut everyone out when he is under extreme stress or needs to find a solution to a problem. A man totally disconnects the part of his brain that controls emotion, goes into problem-solving mode and stops talking. When a man uses the complete shut-out, it can be terrifying for a woman because she only does this when she has been hurt, lied to or abused. A woman assumes that this must also be the case with a man – she must have hurt him and he doesn't love her any more. She tries to encourage him to talk, but he refuses, thinking she doesn't have faith is his ability to solve his problems. When a woman feels hurt, she shuts off and a man thinks she needs space and so he goes to the pub with his friends. If a man completely shuts off, let him do it, he'll be fine. If a woman shuts off, there's trouble brewing and it's time for deep discussion.

Solution: How to Deal With Each Other When You're *Both* Stressed at Christmas

There's no two ways about it: Christmas can be hard on couples, and it's not helped by the fact that you're probably going to spend more time in each other's company than you do for most of the year. In a relationship, partners need to discuss their different ways of dealing with stress. Men need to understand that when a woman talks, she is not expecting him to respond with solutions in order to relieve the stress she's feeling. Women need to understand that when a man doesn't talk, that is not a cue that something is wrong. He needs time on his own. Understanding your different responses to pressure and stress is the best thing a couple can do to help relieve any tensions at Christmas.

Chapter 3

HOW COUPLES CAN WORK TOGETHER AT CHRISTMAS

Your to-do list at Christmas can seem endless. There are cards to be sent, decorations to be put up, presents to be bought and wrapped, and all of that before you realise that you should have made your Christmas cake back in October! It is no surprise that one survey found that 37 per cent of people have to take time off work to finish their Christmas preparations. Then there's all the cooking and hosting to be done on the day itself.

'Mail your packages early so the post office can lose them in time for Christmas.'
JOHNNY CARSON

Naturally, the ideal is for both partners to share pre-Christmas chores, and jobs on the day itself, equally, or to agree between you a strategy that is going to work for you both. Unfortunately, sometimes one partner ends up taking responsibility for most of the preparations and work on the day, and when this happens, it can lead to resentment and frustration.

It may be that in your household the male shoulders more of the responsibility for Christmas, but numerous surveys reveal that women do by far the lion's share of chores and planning at this time of year. Even in those households in which men take most of the responsibility for housework and caring for children over the course of the year, at Christmas women still tend to do more of the planning, decorating and cooking. Say the word 'Christmas' to a man and he is likely to smile and think of Christmas trees and glasses of mulled wine; say it to a woman and she will probably think about shopping, cooking, cleaning, decorations and the 101 other things that have to be done before she can relax. This is not sexist – it's simply a fact that in most relationships, at Christmas women do more of the work.

The number-one reason why couples fall out at Christmas is because women feel that they have to do too much of the work that Christmas entails. The result is resentment and nagging.

At Christmas, the furthest thing from most women's minds is 'goodwill to all men'.

In this chapter, we'll look at how a couple can learn to work together over Christmas and find a way of dealing with things that works for you both. If you can learn to balance what you want and need at this very special time, then not just Christmas but the whole year will be happier and more harmonious.

Why Women Don't Tell You What They Want You to Do

Some men complain that they try to help out at Christmas but feel like they can't get a straight answer about what their wife wants them to do. To men, women often seem vague or to beat around the bush rather than getting to the point. Sometimes a man feels as if he is supposed to guess what she wants, or that he is expected to be a mind-reader. This apparent vagueness is known as indirect speech.

Women's indirect speech has a purpose – it builds relationships with others by avoiding aggression, confrontation or discord. From an evolutionary point of view, being indirect allowed women to avoid disagreement with one another and made it easier to bond by not appearing to be dominant or aggressive. This approach fits perfectly into a woman's overall approach to preserving harmony.

When women use indirect speech with other women, there is seldom a problem – women are sensitive to picking up the real meaning. It can, however, be disastrous when used on men, and is particularly unproductive when planning for Christmas.

Case Study: Barbara and Adam

Barbara was going Christmas shopping with friends and wanted her 16-year-old son, Adam, to clean the kitchen as her family were arriving the next day for Christmas.

'Adam, would you like to clean the kitchen for me, please?' she asked.

'Uh . . . yeah,' was his mumbled response.

When she returned from her trip with her friends, the kitchen still looked like a bomb had hit it. In fact, it was in worse shape than before she'd gone out. She was fuming.

'But I was going to do it before I go out tonight!' Adam complained.

The problem here rested with Barbara. She had used indirect speech and assumed that Adam would realise that when she returned home with her friends, the kitchen would need to be clean. She asked, 'Would you like to clean the kitchen?' No teenage boy would 'like' to clean the kitchen and neither did Adam. A direct request with a deadline like 'Adam, please have the kitchen cleaned before I get home from shopping at midday' would have ensured a more successful outcome.

....

Boys don't 'like' to do household chores —
they need to be directly instructed to do them.

....

With direct instructions there is little room for miscommunication, and males appreciate clear directions. Many women are concerned that direct speech is too aggressive or confronting. When used with another female, that would be true. For males, however, direct talk is perfectly normal because that's how they communicate.

Men's sentences are short, direct, solution-oriented and to the point. This kind of speech helps close business deals quickly and efficiently, and is a means of asserting authority over others.

If a woman wants to have goose instead of turkey for Christmas dinner, she'll say, 'What do you think about having goose on Christmas Day?' A man will usually then give his opinion, rather than agreeing outright. If a man wants goose on Christmas Day, he'll say it directly: 'Let's have goose on Christmas Day this year.' If a woman wants a man to clean the spare room ready for guests arriving, she'll say, 'Do you think you could hoover the spare room at some point?' He would say, 'Will you hoover the spare room, please?' These are the same requests expressed in a different way.

How Indirect Speech Can Lead to a Festive Feud

Judith is tearing her hair out trying to get everything ready in time for Christmas. The kitchen looks like a bomb's hit it, the dishwasher needs unloading, her parents are arriving first thing in the morning, and she hasn't even started wrapping the presents. She wants Mark to help and is annoyed that he hasn't offered, but he doesn't even seem to notice that she is becoming increasingly frantic. Mark suspects that something is wrong, but doesn't know what it is. He comes into the room and says, 'Are you OK, honey?'

Judith replies, 'Yes, fine,' which is indirect talk for 'No, I need you to help me.'

Mark says, 'That's good,' and goes off to watch the rerun of *Octopussy*.

Judith is furious that he hasn't realised she needs his help.

❄

If a man suspects that a woman is stressed or has a problem, he does what men do to other men – he walks away and gives her some space to work things out. She thinks, 'He's uncaring and heartless – he's left me to do everything,' and calls her girlfriends.

When this pattern establishes itself, you can easily see how men and women often fall into arguing at Christmas or how resentment can build. To break this cycle, they both need to understand how the other person thinks and functions.

Solution: How to Talk to a Man

Women need to be direct with men and give them one thing at a time to consider. It may seem difficult at first but with practice it will give you the results you want and you'll have fewer disagreements with the males in your life.

Having a Master's degree in indirect talk, a woman asks 'can' and 'could' questions: 'Can you get the Christmas decorations down from the loft?' A man interprets her words literally so when she asks, 'Can you write the Christmas cards?' he hears, 'Do you have the ability to write Christmas cards?' A man interprets questions beginning with 'can' or 'could' as a check of his ability, so his logical response is yes, he can get the Christmas decorations or he could write Christmas cards but these words carry no commitment to act. Plus, men feel manipulated and forced into giving a 'Yes' response. Ask 'will' or 'would' questions to get commitment. For example, 'Will you buy the Christmas tree tomorrow?' asks for a commitment to tomorrow and a man must answer 'Yes' or 'No'.

You are better off getting a 'No' answer to a 'will you' or 'would you' question and know where you stand than get a 'Yes' to every 'can you' or 'could you' question you ask. A man who asks a woman to marry him says, 'Will you marry me?' He never says, 'Could you marry me?'

Having said that, men don't get let off that easily – they, too, can be masters of indirect speech at Christmas, as these humorous examples show . . .

A Dictionary of the Most Common Male Speech Patterns You'll Hear at Christmas

What he says . . .	What he means . . .
1 'I can't find the brandy butter.'	'I can't see it, it didn't fall into my hands, so it must not exist.'
2 'I thought we weren't doing the present thing this year.'	'I knew you wanted a gift, but I didn't get round to buying it.'
3 'Can I help with Christmas dinner?'	'Why isn't it already on the table?'
4 'There's this great film on on Boxing Day.'	'It's got guns, knives, fast cars and naked women.'
5 'Christmas isn't about material things.'	'I forgot to buy you a Christmas present.'
6 'Oh, socks! Just what I wanted.'	'Where's my real present?'
7 'We're going to be late for the office party.'	'I have a legitimate reason for driving like a maniac.'

8	'Take a break, honey. Christmas is meant to be fun.'	'I can't hear the television over the vacuum-cleaner.'
9	'I thought you deserved something special for Christmas this year.'	'The girl selling jewellery in the department store was a real babe with great curves I wanted to look at close up.'
10	'You know how bad my memory is.'	'I remember the words to the theme song of *Gilligan's Island*, the address of the first girl I kissed and the registration number of every car I've ever owned, but I forgot to buy Brussels sprouts at the supermarket and instead came back with plastic mistletoe and an avocado.'

Why Men Can't Write Christmas Cards and Watch TV

Women are experts at multi-tasking. A woman can be writing a Christmas card list while making mince pies and asking her husband to test the Christmas-tree lights are working. She can have a conversation on the phone while decorating the tree. It's as if a woman is somehow genetically related to the octopus. Most women can do several unrelated things at the same time, and brain scans reveal a woman's brain is never disengaged, it's always active, even when she is asleep. This is the main reason that almost all the world's personal assistants are women. For their jobs, performing a number of different tasks at once is an absolute necessity. Of the 716,148 secretaries in the UK in 1998, 99.1 per cent were women – there were only 5,913 men. Some groups attribute this to girls being groomed for such careers while still at school. That fails to take into account, however, women's domination of organisational and multi-tracking abilities.

Men, on the other hand, find multi-tasking extremely difficult. If a woman asks a man to write Christmas cards while watching TV, he will find it very challenging. If she didn't turn the TV off when she was asking him, he probably won't have even heard her! If he's trying to follow a recipe and you talk to him, he is likely to become angry because he can't follow the written instructions and listen at the same time.

In order to understand why this is, we need to look at how the brain works. The left and right brain hemispheres are connected by a bundle of nerve fibres called the corpus callosum. This cable lets both sides of the brain communicate and exchange information. Try to imagine you have two computers on your shoulders with an interface cable between the two. That cable is the corpus callosum.

Neurologist Roger Gorski of the University of California at Los Angeles confirmed that a woman's brain has a corpus callosum that is 10 per cent thicker than a man's, and has up to 30 per cent more connections between the left and right. He also proved that men and women use different parts of the brain when working on the same task. These findings have since been duplicated by other scientists elsewhere. The available research agrees: men's brains are specialised. Compartmentalised. A male brain is configured to concentrate on one specific, dedicated task at once. In simple terms, it's as though he has little rooms throughout his brain and each room contains at least one main function that operates independently of the rest. This gives him his 'one-thing-at-a-time' approach to everything he does in life. We describe this as 'mono-tracking'.

Research also reveals that the female hormone oestrogen prompts nerve cells to grow more connections within the brain and between the two hemispheres. Studies show the more connections you have, the more fluent your speech. It also explains women's ability to 'multi-track' unrelated activities.

A woman's brain is quite simply configured for doing several unrelated things at the same time.

While men's single-minded, focused approach to everything may seem limiting to women, it allows a man to become a dedicated specialist or expert on one subject. Ninety-six per cent of the world's technical experts are male – they are excellent at performing that one skill.

Solution: How to Get a Man to Listen

Understanding the male 'one-thing-at-a-time' mentality is one of the most important things a woman can ever learn about men, and it is one of the most useful things you can learn if you want a positive response when you ask a man to do something at Christmas. Take an MRI scan of a man's brain when he's reading, and you'll find he is virtually deaf. Remember: you should never talk to a man while he's having a wet shave – unless you mean to hurt him!

If you want to get a man to do something at Christmas – whether it's decorating the tree, serve drinks or anything else – do not ask him when he is in the middle of doing something else, as he won't be able to concentrate on what you are saying to him. Choose your moment carefully and make sure you have his attention. Secondly, only ever give him one thing at a time to do: don't suggest he write Christmas cards while he is watching TV, or talk to him about your plans for Christmas while he is cooking dinner. He needs to focus all his attention on one thing.

If you're still finding it hard to get a man to listen, give him advance notice and provide an agenda. This strategy makes the most impact on a man, because they know what you want to talk about and when. For example, 'I'd like to talk with you about what we're going to buy our parents for Christmas and who we're going to invite. Would after dinner at seven o'clock be a good time for you to talk about it?' This appeals to the logical structure of a man's brain, makes him feel appreciated and passes on the problem! An indirect approach would be 'I'm worried about Christmas – I just don't know how I'm going to get everything done', which creates problems because a man is likely to think that he's being blamed and goes straight on the defensive. Men need timetables, agendas, bottom-line answers and deadlines.

Why Women Talk About So Many Things At Once

If a man asks a woman directly at Christmas what she wants him to do, she will usually respond with a long list of chores that need to be done – including things she plans to do herself – and then she'll throw in something completely unrelated: 'Well, there's the turkey to be ordered and collected. Then I need to get a gift for Celia – I'll go to the shopping centre tomorrow. If you could get the Christmas tree, that would be great. Oh, did you remember to return your boss's call? Then there's the lights to go in the tree in the garden and . . .' As a result, men usually have no idea what a woman wants them to do.

In women, speech is a specific area located primarily in the front left hemisphere with another, smaller specific area in the right hemisphere. Having speech on both sides of the brain makes women good conversationalists. They enjoy it, and do lots of it. As we learned, women also have a greater flow of information between left and right hemispheres. These two functions not only enable women to do several different things at once, but also to *talk* about several subjects simultaneously – sometimes in a single sentence. It's like juggling three or four balls at the one time, and most women seem to do it effortlessly.

For males, speech and language are not critical brain skills. They operate mainly in the left brain and have no specific location. When a male talks, MRI scans show that his entire left hemisphere becomes active as it searches to find a centre for speaking, but is unable to find much. Consequently, men aren't much good at talking. Men evolved as lunch-chasers, remember, not communicators. The hunt was conducted with a series of non-verbal signals and often the hunters would sit for hours silently watching for their prey. They didn't talk or bond.

Women's ability to multi-track – or change subject – is frustrating for a man as the male brain is mono-tracked and can only handle one subject at a time. A woman may start talking about decorating the tree, switch in mid-sentence to what to eat on Christmas Eve and then, without any warning, revert back to the first subject with a little bit of something completely different dropped in for good measure. Men become perplexed and befuddled, and women find it baffling that men can't follow their conversations. At Christmas, when there is so much going on in all our lives and so much to talk about, women's ability to multi-track seems to reach new heights.

A woman might be telling you about her day at work in one sentence and then, in the next, say, 'That reminds me – can you write the Christmas cards tonight so we can get them sent off tomorrow?' Switching subjects is very confusing to men, but perfectly straightforward for other women to follow.

Solution: How to Put Things to a Man in Simple Terms

If you multi-track several subjects with a man, he gets lost. It's important for a woman to understand that you should present only one clear thought or idea at a time. Don't ask him to pick up a Christmas present for your daughter after he's finished work in the middle of a conversation about what you're going to do for New Year's. It may seem like a logical progression to you, but his brain won't be able to process the switch of subject. Choose your timing carefully and put it to him in simple terms.

....

The first rule of talking to a man: keep it simple!
Give him only one thing at a time to think about.

....

When Christmas Becomes a Nag

What if a woman has asked her partner directly for help with Christmas preparations but he still isn't helping out? What if she has avoided asking him to do too many things at once, has not used indirect speech and has given him a clear request? The outcome is usually that she asks him again, and again, and again, and hopes that at some point he will listen. She ends up nagging him and Christmas can turn into a tug of war.

Nag: (verb) to annoy, badger, bend someone's ear, berate, breathe down someone's neck, worry, harass, hassle, henpeck, pester, plague, provoke, scold, torment; (noun) a person, especially a woman, who nags.

'Nagging' is a term used almost exclusively by men to describe women.

Many men complain that their wives nag them incessantly at Christmas. Most women deny they nag. They see themselves as reminding the males in their lives to do the things that must be done: at Christmas, that could be household chores, checking the Christmas lights are still working and picking up the turkey from the shop. Some nagging is considered constructive. Where would many men be without a woman in their lives cajoling them not to drink too much beer and eat too much Christmas pudding and make sure they take a walk on Christmas Day? Nagging can take place at any time of year, but at Christmas, when there is simply so much to do and so much going on, men often say that their wives' nagging reaches a new level.

....

Nagging can reach fever pitch at Christmas, the most stressful time of the year.

....

If men nag, however, that's viewed very differently by society. Men are not naggers. They're assertive, they're leaders, and invariably they're passing on their wisdom – and gently reminding women of the path to take if they happen to forget along the way. Sure, they criticise, find fault, moan and complain, but it's always for the woman's benefit. The repetition of their advice, like 'We get lost every time we visit my sister. Read the map before you set off! How many times must I tell you?' and 'Can't you dress up a bit more to the Christmas office party? My boss is going to be there' shows admirable persistence and, above all, shows that they care.

Women, similarly, feel that nagging shows that they care, but men rarely see it in the same light. A woman will chide a man about eating all the mince pies, leaving his opened Christmas presents scattered around the house and not remembering to take out the rubbish. She knows she's being irritating, but believes the way to get through to a man is by repeating, over and over, the same instructions until they one day, hopefully, sink in. But usually, when a woman starts repeating her orders, the male brain hears only one thing: nagging. Like a dripping tap, nagging wears away at his soul and can gradually build a simmering resentment. Men everywhere put nagging at the top of the list of their pet hates. And it's the one thing that's sure to ruin Christmas for everyone.

Why Do Women Nag So Much at Christmas?

Nagging occurs between people who are intimately connected – wives, husbands, mothers, sons, daughters and live-in partners. That's why the stereotypical nagger, the nagger of comic routines, is a wife or mother – those who are tied down with domestic responsibilities, who feel generally powerless in life, frustrated and who feel unable to change their lives in an upfront, direct way.

Women often display this kind of frustration at Christmas, when they feel the weight of the responsibility of making sure everyone has a good time. They frequently shoulder the burden of writing Christmas cards, buying presents, cleaning the house ready for everyone arriving, food shopping and cooking, and end up feeling that everyone else is enjoying themselves while they are 'slaving away'.

She can end up stomping around in a confused, suppressed rage, feeling increasingly frustrated that no one else realises how much she is doing for them. She knows she has as much right to enjoy Christmas as everyone else, but she doesn't know what to do about it.

Centuries of stereotyping, family attitudes, women's magazines, movies and television commercials have convinced her the role a truly womanly woman prefers is that of Perfect Wife and Mother, and she believes this is never more important than at Christmas. She has to create the perfect home, have the perfect decorations, give perfect presents, cook the perfect meal and in short be a festive domestic goddess. Christmas cookery programmes starring women as the perfect Christmas hostess surely haven't helped. She has become brainwashed into trying to live by a 'truth' she knows may no longer be appropriate. She doesn't want the epitaph on her grave to read, 'She had the best Christmas wreath in the street,' but she doesn't know how to break free.

Why Women Place Such Importance on Christmas

Women place a high value on the home and family. In one survey, most women who worked said that if money was no object, they would prefer to be a homemaker or 'lady of leisure' than have a career. In a similar survey in Australia, careers only rated a top priority for 5 per cent of women aged 18–65. Across the board, 80 per cent of all women put raising their children in traditional families at the top of their priority list. Whether a woman works or not, the family and children are very important to them. It is no surprise that at Christmastime most women try to become the perfect mother, wife and hostess.

As nest-defenders, women's overwhelming urge is to be liked by others. They've always been the nurturers of relationships – with partners, children and other family or social groups. Their brains are organised to succeed in making relationships work. Christmas is the ideal opportunity for women to demonstrate their capabilities as wife, mother and all-round domestic goddess and to work on nurturing relationships.

The Christmas Fairy and the Naughty Little Elf

Some women view men as naughty little boys who never grew up. They sometimes feel they are the only sensible adult in the family. In a man's working environment he can communicate, problem-solve and produce positive outcomes and, indeed, gets paid significantly more than the women doing the same jobs. His female partner knows he has these skills, so thus gets enormously frustrated that he doesn't seem to use them at home. In December, she feels things get infinitely worse. She is the Christmas Fairy – making sure that everything is magical and runs smoothly, and he becomes the Naughty Little Elf, leaving mince-pie crumbs and empty glasses all over the house. He's on holiday from work, and she may well be, too, but her workload has doubled.

The trouble is that the woman is then tempted to treat her partner more as a naughty little boy than as a capable man. His reaction, as a result, is to start behaving like one. This shift in attitude is a start along the precarious path of depreciating the relationship. The more the man rebels, the more the woman nags. The more he resists, the more she starts to act like his mother. Eventually, they both reach a point where they no longer see each other as partners, lovers and best friends. And there's no greater passion-killer for the man than starting to feel he's with his mother, or for the woman than feeling she's with an immature, selfish and lazy little boy.

How the Nagger Feels

Women know they nag, but that doesn't mean they enjoy it. Usually they're only doing it as a means to an end. They want their husbands to spontaneously offer to cook Christmas dinner, they want them to empty the rubbish bin and think about whether there are enough clean towels to go round for their guests – in short, they want them to take some of the responsibility for making sure Christmas is a success.

Some women have turned nagging into an art form. We have identified five basic nags that take place at Christmas:

The Single-Subject Nag: 'Kurt, how about getting the decorations down from the loft?' A pause. 'Kurt, you said you'd get the decorations down.' Another five minutes later. 'What about the decorations, Kurt? The tree doesn't decorate itself, you know.'

The Multi-Nag: 'There are pine needles all over the floor in the sitting room, Nigel, the spare bed needs changing, and you need to put a nail in the front door for the wreath. When are you going to fix the Christmas lights? And . . .' etc., etc.

The Beneficial Nag: 'Have you taken your pills today, Ray? And stop eating that Christmas cake – it's bad for your cholesterol and weight . . .'

The Third-Party Nag: 'Well, Moira says Shane has already done their Christmas shopping and written their cards. It will be Christmas Eve before you know it.'

The Advance Nag: 'Well, I hope you're going to watch your drinking tonight at the office party, Dale. We don't want a repeat of last year's fiasco.'

Usually, women laugh hardest at these descriptions. They recognise themselves and their words, but still they see no real alternative. They think that if they want a successful family Christmas, they either have to accept that they have to do everything themselves or they have to nag.

When nagging gets out of hand, the nagger's relationships with others can really suffer. Men may ignore her even more, which will only fuel her irritation and, sometimes, rage. She may end up feeling alone and may become resentful and miserable. This is the last thing you want at Christmas. When it gets out of hand, it's been known to destroy relationships completely.

How the Victim Feels

From a male standpoint, nagging is a continual, indirect, negative reminder about the things he hasn't done, or about his shortcomings. It's Christmas and the whole point of Christmas is to have a relaxed time with family and enjoy the day.

The more the nagger nags, the more the victim retreats behind the kind of defensive barriers that drive the nagger crazy – he might watch the TV, or play games with the kids, or go to the pub. No one likes being on the receiving end of subdued rage, ambiguous messages, self-pity and blame or having guilt continually thrust at them. Everyone avoids the nagger, leaving her alone and feeling resentful. When she starts feeling even more trapped, unrecognised and isolated – stuck in the kitchen worrying about whether the turkey is going to be dry while the rest of the family share a glass of mulled wine in the sitting room – the victim may suffer even more.

Why Nagging Never Works

The main reason nagging doesn't work is that it has built-in expectations of failure. While naggers hope their words will push their victims into action, they often expect them to fail or they invite a negative response.

Their major mistake is the way they approach the problem. Instead of saying, 'I expect this as my right,' they say, 'Why do you always leave everything to me at Christmas? Do I have to do everything around here?' They make feeble, indirect requests that are heavily laden with guilt. The 'requests' usually come in random groups that are framed in indirect speech, which male brains have limited ability to decode. For a male, it's like being continually bitten by a plague of mosquitoes. He gets small, itchy bites all over and can't seem to swat them. 'This is my Christmas too, you know . . . I spend my Christmas holiday working my fingers to the bone to make this place look nice for *your* family while you just sit there watching the television . . .'

This kind of nagging is pointless, self-defeating and creates a lose-lose situation. With this approach, nagging becomes a corrosive habit that causes great stress, disharmony, resentment and anger. This isn't how either of you wants to spend Christmas.

How to Understand a Nagger – Why Women Want to Feel Valued at Christmas

If a victim is honest with himself and admits the elements of truth in the nagging and recognises that nagging is usually a cry for recognition, he could quickly turn the situation into a win-win. The greatest urge in human nature is to feel important.

Nagging is a sign that a woman wants more: more recognition from her family for what she has given so far, and more opportunities to move on to something better.

'Every Christmas my mum goes on about how much hard work she's put into it – everything she does, she just has to make a point about it,' sighs Ian, a constantly nagged teenager. 'When she makes a table decoration, she tells us how long it took her to make it. When she's made her own bread sauce, she makes some loaded little comment to draw attention to it. I'd rather she didn't do it in the end. Why can't we just enjoy Christmas without her going on about every little thing?'

She goes on about 'every little thing' because it's hard to feel confident and powerful if you feel that nobody has noticed what you've achieved. It is because her tasks are so unappreciated that Adam's mother nags at him for recognition. If Adam gave her some of the recognition she craves – and deserves – the quality of his life would dramatically improve. Giving the nagger recognition for performing small, routine tasks eliminates most nagging.

Because the basis of nagging is truth, the victim must accept equal responsibility for nagging. Nagging is the result of poor communication.

The Challenge for the Victim and for the Nagger

To achieve a win-win situation, both parties must want to change and share the responsibility. The victim needs to recognise and accept his contribution to the problem. Victims develop patterns of avoidance, which compound matters. If your wife nags you at Christmas, you may ignore her, go to the pub with your family, make excuses or even shout her down. Some men even go into work over Christmas or return to work early to avoid their wives. Victims get it easy because they can always blame the nagger. But the only way out is for the victim to stop, take stock of themselves and consider their contribution. They should see nagging as a cry for help. Ask yourself whether you recognise how much work the other person has put into Christmas. Do you understand why they may feel frustrated? How can you help? Ask yourself whether you want the other person to have a happy Christmas.

If you are a nagger, have you thought that the other person may be unable to meet your request? Are you behaving like a parent towards them? Do you insist on instant action, regardless of the needs of the other person at the time? Do you continually repeat your demands?

If your answer to any of these questions is 'Yes', sit down with the other person and tell them what is frustrating you, agree to a time frame for your requests, stop repeating yourself, state your needs, then stop and listen to the response of your spouse. Avoid 'you' statements, which cause resistance from the other person. Communication really is the key to a happy Christmas.

Kids at Christmas – How to Get Them to Do What You Want Without Nagging

Part of responsible parenting is to remind, persuade and even demand that children behave in a certain way for their own safety, well-being and success in life. We want them to have a great time at Christmas – every parent wants that – but at the same time, they still have to abide by certain rules. When they're on holiday from school at Christmas and we're all in a confined space together, it's easy to turn to nagging – 'Cameron, how many times have I told you to put your presents in your room? Cameron, are you listening to me?' or 'Gemma, will you stop playing with that computer game and lay the table? I'm not going to ask you again.'

And who's to blame for a constantly nagging parent in the home – the disobedient child, or the nagging parent? The answer is – the parent.

The parent has conditioned the child to automatically respond the way they do. The child has been taught it's not necessary to respond after the first request and that your standard is for you to remind, persuade or demand several times before you expect them to comply. The child has trained you to keep repeating your demands and they think you don't really want them to act.

As a parent, this is a vicious circle. The more you repeat yourself and complain, the longer the child will resist. The more frustrated you become with the child's non-compliance, the angrier you get and the louder you become. The child now starts to resent your anger because, in their mind, they have not done anything wrong. Now the child becomes confused and frustrated.

Solution: How to Get Your Family in Training for Christmas

If you find you are continually nagging someone, whether it is your partner or your child, it shows that person has trained you to do what they want you to do. In other words, they are making the rules and you are complying. Let's say they keep leaving wet towels on the bathroom floor. All year you ask them to pick them up, but at Christmas, when you have guests staying who are also using the bathroom, you find you are repeating yourself continually and becoming very frustrated. The reality here is that the other person knows that you will eventually pick up the towels anyway – all they have to do is put up with a little nagging from you, which is probably a small price to pay. So, you have been trained by them.

Training someone to do what you want is the same whether they are a child or an adult. You reward the behaviour you want and ignore the behaviour you don't want. For example, in the case of the wet towels, the next time it happens you place the wet towel out of sight in the bottom of a broom cupboard. When the offender goes to have their next shower, they will ask you where it is and you give them the towel's coordinates. They will then discover how uncomfortable it is to dry themselves with a damp, smelly towel. It's also easier to pick up their towel than have to ask where it is. It only takes two or three times for them to become trained in picking up and hanging their towel. The same technique works well for dirty socks, underwear or any item that you don't want left around. With this technique, you become the trainer and not the trainee and nagging will no longer be necessary. If, however, you choose to continue to pick up after everyone, you will have chosen to remain the trained person and so lose the right to nag anyone about leaving mess on the floor.

The key is to avoid being sarcastic, judgemental or aggressive, as this usually has an opposite effect, particularly on males. Similarly, if someone leaves wrapping paper or unopened presents around the house and they're getting in the way, tell them you will put them in a cupboard or drawer. Do not put them in their room, workshop or any place that is convenient, as that will simply reinforce the behaviour you don't want. If you want to retrain someone, you must resist the urge to pick up after them.

When a man puts his own things away, reward him for his contribution with a smile or thanks. Some women are appalled by the thought of thanking a man for doing something as basic as picking up his own clothes, but it's important to understand that men did not evolve as nest-defenders and general tidiness is not something that comes naturally to them. If a man's mother didn't train him to do these things, it will be up to you to train him.

Naturally, it will take a little while to retrain the individuals in your life, so start early and by Christmas you will see the benefits. The key is always to manage the males in your life, rather than arguing, becoming angry, or feeling frustrated with them. That way, both sexes will be able to live happily ever after.

Women's Secret Point-Scoring System at Christmas

Sometimes, though, difficulties in managing the workload at Christmas and in a couple's relationship have nothing to do with nagging . . .

❄

Andrew and Karen had everything going for them. Andrew had a great job, they had recently moved into a new home, their two kids were happy and well balanced, they just had their first family Christmas and had had a full house for Christmas Day.

Behind the scenes, however, the run-up to Christmas had been marred with bickering and nit-picking. Christmas Day itself had been tense. Karen barely said a word to Andrew and he had spent most of the day playing with the kids and in the evening had gone to the pub with his father. It had been a disaster. Even though they really loved each other, they were both confused, upset and worried. Karen seemed to have spent all Christmas being angry, while Andrew was bewildered – he just didn't understand what was happening.

The problem was that Andrew, like most men, was completely unaware that Karen was using a special female scoring system to rate their marriage.

Karen felt that Andrew worked too hard – he had worked right up until Christmas Eve and went into the office for a few days after Christmas, even though no one else was going in. She felt she had had to do all the planning for Christmas on her own. Christmas was about the kids and being with family, but Andrew didn't seem to care. Eventually, in the New Year, they were desperate to understand what had become of their relationship, so they went to a counsellor and had the following conversation:

KAREN: 'He works all the time. I barely saw him over
    Christmas. It was our first Christmas at home. I need a
    man who wants me, looks after me and participates in
    the family without me having to nag him to do so.'
ANDREW: (amazed) 'I can't believe what you're saying, Karen
    . . . What do you mean I don't look after you and
    the kids? Look at our beautiful home, the lovely presents
    I bought for everyone, the great food we ate . . . I provide
    all this for you and the kids! I worked so hard up to
    Christmas so that we could have the sort of day we wanted
    and you don't even appreciate it!'
KAREN: (angrily) 'You just don't get it, do you, Andrew? I
    don't think you ever will! I did everything for you over
    Christmas . . . I cooked Christmas dinner, cleaned and
    decorated the house before everyone came, bought all the
    presents . . . All you did was work, mess around with the
    kids, eat and watch TV. You didn't even unload the dish-
    washer or help me put up the tree. Tell me one thing you
    did to help me over Christmas . . . Tell me the last time
    you said you loved me.'
ANDREW: (shocked) 'Karen . . . you know I love you . . .'

Most men are totally unaware that women keep a point score on their partner's overall performance in a relationship or at Christmas. Most men are oblivious to the fact that this scoring system even exists and can fall foul of it without ever understanding where they've gone wrong. The number of points a man accrues from his partner directly affects the quality of his life at any time. Not only do women keep score, they also own the scoreboard! When a man and woman decide to live together, they never discuss the finer detail of what each will contribute to the relationship. And when couples spend their first Christmas at home, they never discuss who will do what.

Men See Only the Big Picture

Men prefer to stand back and see the 'big picture' and make a smaller number of big contributions than be bogged down with a series of what seem like smaller, less important ones. For example, a man may not often present his partner with a gift but at Christmas, he'll buy a big one. Women's brains, on the other hand, are organised for fine detail and they make a wider range of smaller decisions on the many intricate facets of a working relationship. A woman would rather a man bought a smaller present for Christmas and then surprise her with other smaller presents during the course of the year than spend a lot of money on just buying a big Christmas present.

If a man drives to his in-laws on Boxing Day, he gets one point. If he peels the vegetables on Christmas morning or tells her he loves her, he also gets one point each. In other words, the points are given for the number of actions taken, not for the size, quality or outcome of a single action. Ninety-five per cent of all points awarded in a relationship are for everyday things that do or don't happen. It truly is the thought that counts with women. This difference is the cause of many misunderstandings between men and women, and many arguments at Christmas.

Our Experiment With Peter and Alison

Peter was a finance broker who worked long hours seeing clients and building his business. His wife, Alison, kept house and cared for their two kids. The four of them were spending Christmas at home. They described themselves as a happy, normal couple and said they generally enjoyed Christmas, but Alison said that she felt she did a lot more of the work, while Peter said he thought it was roughly even. They kept a scorecard daily for two weeks over Christmas of the contributions they believed they made to their relationship, and to allocate the number of points they believed should be received from the other. One point would be allocated for a minor contribution and a maximum of 30 points for a major contribution to the relationship. They should also record penalty points for things their partner did that irritated them. They were not to discuss with each other how, or when, points were allocated, or which activities had scored points, if any.

Here are some examples of how Peter scored over that Christmas period.

How Peter Scored at Christmas

	He	She
Getting decorations from loft	3	1
Buying and putting up the Christmas tree	3	2
Hanging wreath on door	2	1
Delivering Christmas cards to neighbours	3	1
Checking fairy lights and replacing faulty ones	3	1
Telling her she looked beautiful when they went to a party	1	3
Carving turkey	1	1

	He	She
Assembling model plane for his son on Christmas Day	5	1
Playing a board game with the kids on Christmas Day	3	2
Take out rubbish	1	1
Bought necklace for Christmas present	10	3
Driving to in-laws' on Boxing Day	5	1
Going into work on 27 December	5	0
Taking down Christmas tree	5	2

Things Alison Scored That Weren't on Peter's List

	She
Giving me his coat when it was cold	3
Sharpening carving knife	1
Tidying up used wrapping paper in sitting room	1
Serving drinks to guests	1
Opening tight jar	1
Making buck's fizz	1
Complimenting me on Christmas dinner	3
Staying with me at his office party when I didn't know anyone	2

Things Peter Could Have Done to Earn More Points

	She
Go Christmas shopping with me	5
Write Christmas cards	2
Offer to clean kitchen on Christmas Eve	2
Peel vegetables	1

Set dining table	1
Do the washing-up on Christmas Day	2
Kiss me under mistletoe	1
Kiss me under mistletoe without groping	3
Not flick remote control	2
Make me feel more important than the children	3
Unload dishwasher	1

These lists point out several things: first, because men have spatially oriented brains they allocate more points than women for physical and spatially related tasks. For example, Peter gave himself five points for helping his son construct his Christmas present, but Alison only saw it as earning one point. For him, it had been a difficult but skilful task and he was proud of what he had achieved; for her, it had been playing with a toy. Women usually award a man one point for each domestic task he performs but are more likely to allocate more points for small, personal or intimate tasks than for large tasks. For instance, when Peter told Alison that Christmas dinner was delicious, she gave him three points but he was totally unaware he'd scored any at all. It's not that he forgot about it; it simply never occurred to him that complimenting a woman's cooking was a good point-scorer. When he bought her an expensive necklace for Christmas, he thought he'd earned at least ten points, but she only gave him three points.

Peter thought that working over Christmas was a positive because it was something he didn't want to do but he was providing for his family; Alison thought he was neglecting them and cared more about work than about the family, so she gave him no points. She was probably tempted to deduct them. If he had called her from work to say he loved her and missed her, and called again when he was nearly home, he would have scored at least three points. Like most men, Peter was oblivious to the fact that little things mean a lot to a woman, particularly at Christmas, despite having often heard it from his mother and grandmother.

How Alison Scored at Christmas

The list of Alison's personal activities was four times longer than Peter's. She had written out every activity in detail but only allocated low scores to most. Doing the Christmas food shop, sending Christmas cards, going to the post office to send a Christmas present, making up the bed in the spare room, buying Christmas decorations, making a wreath for the front door, making a table decoration, visiting an elderly neighbour, planning family get-togethers, putting up the children's Christmas stockings and reading *The Night Before Christmas* to them scored one point each. Repetitive actions such as washing clothes and cooking all scored one point each time she did them.

Penalty Points

Penalty points are deducted whenever one partner does something that frustrates or annoys the other. They both gave each other very few penalty points – but it was Christmas after all!

Penalty Points Alison Gave Peter
Getting drunk at the Christmas office party	-6
Telling a rude joke on Christmas Day	-5

Penalty Points Peter Gave Alison
Talking to me while I watched TV	-2
Nagging me to take the Christmas tree down	-5

Peter's complaints were about things Alison did or didn't do for him, while Alison's complaints were more about things Peter did in public.

Alison and Peter's Reactions

At the end of the experiment, Peter had given himself an average weekly score of 62 points. He gave Alison a weekly average of 60 points, so he felt happy the relationship score was evenly balanced. Alison had scored herself an average of 78 points but had only given Peter a weekly average of 48 points.

Alison felt the score was weighted 30 points a week in Peter's favour. This explained a resentment simmering inside her at Christmas. Peter was devastated at the result. He had been proceeding as if everything was just fine and enjoying Christmas to the full, but had no idea how Alison was feeling.

For Peter and Alison, this experiment was an eye-opener. What had begun as a simple fun test to show how men and women score points differently and rate each other's contribution to Christmas had shown how hard Alison worked over Christmas and how she carried resentment that Peter was at work when he should be around his family. Peter had thought he was bringing 'home the bacon' and that his hard work enabled them to have a good Christmas. They resolved that next Christmas Peter would book more time off work and they would try to manage the jobs for Christmas in a way that made both of them equally happy.

Take the Test Now

This Christmas, with your partner, score and record all your contributions to your relationship for two weeks. Evaluate the results, and you can use them as a template to approach not only next Christmas but your entire relationship in ways that will give you more happiness than you ever imagined. A score difference of less than 15 per cent shows a fairly even relationship where no one feels resentful or used. A difference of 15 per cent to 30 per cent shows enough misunderstanding to cause tension, and more than 30 per cent means someone feels unhappy in the relationship.

The partner with the negative score needs to balance their contribution by doing things their mate likes to even the score and reduce tension. The result will be a more contented relationship and a happier Christmas.

Chapter 4

WHY WE DRIVE EACH OTHER ROUND THE BEND AT CHRISTMAS

Most couples have to spend long periods of time in the car during the festive season. Even if you are spending Christmas Day at home, you may well have to drive to parties, visit relatives at the other end of the country, shuttle guests and children from one place to another and drive to the local shopping centre or supermarket. Packed motorways, heaving shopping-centre car parks and driving to unfamiliar locations all place stress on a couple. In fact, some couples feel like they spend half of the Christmas holidays trying to find their way to friends' houses, attempting to locate that elusive parking space and then trying to find their car after they've done the Christmas shopping.

....

Two-thirds of drivers quarrel with passengers while on the move. Happy Christmas!

....

Family tensions that have been simmering in the close confines of the festive home can come to a head once behind the wheel. In fact, in-car disputes during the seasonal get-away are such an issue that the phenomenon has been given its own term – Festive Auto Tension (FAT).

....

Festive Auto Tension is a recognised condition caused by the stress of Christmas driving.

....

Sometimes it feels like women and men are biologically programmed to argue when put in a car together. And in a way they are. But why is this, and what can we do about it? As we will show in this chapter, the vast majority of arguments when driving at Christmas stem from two basic problems: women aren't very good at reading maps, and men won't ask for directions.

Problem 1 – How a Car Drive Nearly Ruined Christmas Eve

It's Christmas Eve and John and Ruth are driving to a friend's party in an unfamiliar area. According to the directions, it should have taken them 20 minutes. It has already taken them 50 and there is still no sign of their destination. John is becoming grumpy, and Ruth started feeling despondent when they passed the same garage for the third time. John is driving. He always drives. They never discuss why he always drives, he just does. And, like most men, he becomes a different person behind the wheel.

John asks Ruth to look up the address in the street directory. She opens it at the appropriate page and then turns the directory upside down. She rotates it to the right way up and then turns it upside down again. Then she sits silently and stares at it. She understands what a map means, but when it comes to applying it to where they are going, it seems strangely irrelevant. It's like studying geography in school. All those pink and green shapes bear little resemblance to the real world in which she lives. Sometimes she copes with the map when they are heading north, but south is a disaster – and they are heading south. She rotates the map one more time. After several more seconds of silence, John speaks.

'Stop turning the map upside down!' he snaps.

'But I need to face it in the direction we're going,' Ruth explains meekly.

'Yeah, but you can't read it upside down!' John barks.

'Look, John, it makes logical sense to face the map in the direction we need to go. That way, I can match the street signs with the directory!' she says, raising her voice indignantly.

'Yeah, but if the map was supposed to be read upside down, they'd print the writing upside down, right? Stop fooling around and tell me where to go!'

'I'll tell you where to go all right!' responds Ruth furiously. She throws the street directory at him and shouts, 'Read it yourself!'

❄

Does this argument sound familiar? It's one of the most common between men and women of all races, stretching back thousands of years. In the eleventh century, Lady Godiva rode her horse naked down the wrong Coventry Street, Juliet got lost trying to get back home after a love tryst with Romeo, Cleopatra threatened Marc Antony with castration for trying to force her to understand his battle maps, and the Wicked Witch of the West often headed south, north or east.

So Why Do We Always Get Lost at Christmas?

Reading maps and understanding where you are relies on spatial ability. Brain scans show that spatial ability is located mostly in the right brain for men and boys, and is one of a male's strongest abilities. It developed from ancient times to allow men, the hunters, to calculate the speed, movement and distance of prey, work out how fast they had to run to catch their targets, and know how much force they needed to kill their lunch with a rock or a spear. Spatial ability is located in both brain hemispheres for women but does not have a specific measurable location as it does in males. Only about 10 per cent of women have spatial abilities that are as dynamic as those of the best men. The majority of women have limited spatial ability. This is not sexist – there are plenty of things that women do better than men, but in this case biology has given men the clear advantage.

Spatial ability means being able to picture in the mind the shape of things, their dimensions, coordinates, proportions, movement and geography. It also involves being able to imagine an object being rotated in space, navigating around an obstacle course and seeing things from a three-dimensional perspective. Its purpose is to work out the movement of a target and know how to hit it.

Spatial ability is not strong in women and girls because being able to chase animals and find the way home was never part of a woman's job description. This is why many women have trouble reading a map or street directory and why you always end up arguing when visiting friends and relatives at Christmas.

....

Women don't have good spatial skills because they evolved chasing little else besides men.

....

There are thousands of documented scientific studies that confirm male superiority in spatial skills. This is not surprising considering his evolution as a hunter. But modern man no longer has to catch lunch. Today, he uses his spatial ability in other areas such as golf, computer games and any sport or activity involving chasing something or aiming at a target. Most women think hunting is boring. But if they had a specific right brain area for aiming at a target, they would not only enjoy it, they would succeed.

Why Santa Knows Where to Go

Santa Claus is probably so good at navigating his way to all those children's houses because he's male. The fact is, visiting relatives and friends at Christmas would be a lot easier if men navigated. Spatial ability allows a man to rotate a map in his mind and know in which direction to go. Most males can read a map while facing north and know that they need to go south. Similarly, most males can read a map and then successfully navigate by memory. Studies show that a man's brain measures speed and distance to know when to change direction. If put in an unfamiliar room with no windows, most men can point north. As a lunch-chaser, he needed to find his way back home or there would be little chance of survival.

Father Christmas must be male because he can successfully navigate his way to so many children's homes.

Why Women Get Lost in the Multi-Storey Car Park

Sit in any sports stadium and you can witness how men leave their seats to buy a drink and successfully navigate their way back to that seat some time later. Go to any city in the world and watch female tourists standing at junctions furiously turning their maps round and looking lost. Visit a multi-storey car park at any shopping centre at Christmastime and watch female shoppers wandering around gloomily with their Christmas presents trying to find their car. If a man has to return to the same location at a later time – e.g. finding his car in the shopping-centre car park – he can find it easily because his spatial area can store the information.

How Women Can Navigate

'If men didn't design maps that way, we wouldn't have to turn them upside down,' many women complain. The British Cartography Society, however, reports that 50 per cent of its members are female and that 50 per cent of those who design and edit maps are also women. 'Map design is a two-dimensional task in which women are equally as capable as men,' said leading British cartographer Alan Collinson. 'The difficulty that most women have is reading and navigating with the map because they need a three-dimensional perspective to navigate a route. I design tourist maps that have a three-dimensional perspective – they show trees, mountains and other landmarks. Women have much greater success with this type of map. Our tests show that men have the ability to turn a two-dimensional map into a three-dimensional view in their mind, but most women don't seem to be able to do this.' Women dramatically improve their navigational skills using perspective maps.

Three-dimensional maps could help resolve a lot of in-car disputes over the Christmas period.

Another interesting finding has been that men score highly when navigating with a group leader who verbally tells them new directions at each point on a given route. Women, by contrast, perform abysmally when given verbal instructions. This shows how men can convert sound signals into three-dimensional mind maps to visualise the correct direction and route to take, whereas women perform better with a three-dimensional perspective map.

How to Have a Happy Christmas in the Car

Men love to drive fast around winding roads because their spatial skills come into play – gear ratios, clutch and brake combinations, relative speed to corners, angles and distances. And they do it with the radio turned off.

The modern male driver sits behind the wheel, hands his wife a map and asks her to navigate. With her limited spatial ability, she becomes silent and starts turning the map round and feels incompetent. Then she tries to identify something on the horizon that resembles something on the map. Most men don't understand that if you don't have specific areas in the brain for mental map rotation, you'll rotate it in your hands. It makes perfect sense to a woman to face a map in the direction she is travelling. For a man to avoid arguments at Christmas, he should avoid asking a woman to read a map.

....

To have a happy Christmas, never insist
that a woman read a map or street directory.

....

Having spatial ability on both sides of the brain interferes with a female's speech function, so if you give a woman a street directory, she'll stop talking before she turns it round. Give it to a man and he'll continue talking – but he'll also turn the radio off because he can't operate his hearing functions at the same time as his map-reading skills. That's why when a phone rings in his home he demands that everyone keeps quiet while he answers it.

Christmas Driving – Who Should Go Behind the Wheel?

Short days and long nights around Christmas can make driving a little more challenging. It's likely you'll be driving in the dark, so who should drive? While a woman can see better in the dark than a man, especially at the red end of the spectrum, a man's eyes allow for better long-distance vision over a narrower field, which gives him much better – and therefore safer – long-distance night vision than a woman. Combined with his spatial ability, a man can separate and identify the movement of other vehicles on the road ahead and behind. Most women can testify to what is a kind of night blindness: the inability to distinguish which side of the road approaching traffic is on. This is a task that a man's hunting vision is equipped to handle. This means that if you are going on a long driving trip – perhaps to visit relatives at the other end of the country – it makes sense for a woman to drive during the day and for a man to drive at night. Women can see more detail in the dark than men but only over a shorter, wider field.

If you're driving a long way at Christmas, men should drive at night and women should drive in the day.

What If She's Driving to the Christmas Party?

Men all around the world give the same instructions to women: 'Turn left . . . Slow down! Change gear . . . Watch out for those pedestrians . . . Concentrate . . . Stop crying!' For a man, driving is a test of his spatial ability relative to the environment. For a woman, the purpose of driving is to get safely from point A to point B. If a woman is driving at Christmas – or at any time of year – a man's best strategy as a passenger is to close his eyes, turn up the radio and stop commentating because, overall, women are safer drivers than men. She'll get him there – it may just take a little longer, that's all. But at least he can relax and arrive alive.

....

On average, women clock up an extra 203 miles at Christmas. Over a quarter of the miles are for Christmas shopping, and 41 per cent are racked up on visiting family and friends.

....

A woman will criticise a man's driving because his spatial ability allows him to make decisions and judgements that look dangerous to her. Provided he doesn't have a poor driving record, she also needs to relax and not criticise, and just let him do the driving.

How to Give Directions to a Woman

Never give a woman directions like 'Head north' or 'Go west for five kilometres' as this requires compass skills. Instead, give directions involving landmarks such as 'Drive past McDonald's and head for the building with the National Bank sign on top.' This allows a woman to pick up these landmarks with her peripheral vision. Builders and architects everywhere lose millions in business deals by presenting two-dimensional plans and blueprints to female decision-makers. A man's brain can convert the plan to three dimensions to see how the building would look completed, but to a woman it's just a page of irrelevant lines. A three-dimensional model or computer image will sell houses to women. With this information, a woman need never again feel like an idiot when looking at a map. Give it to a man, it's his job.

It's much more relaxing for a man to navigate and drive while a woman talks about the interesting landmarks and sights along the way. A man has inferior verbal skills compared with a woman, so his navigational skills seem like a fair trade-off. It means that he can find his way to the address of his friend's Christmas party, even if he won't know what to say when he gets there.

Parking at Christmas – the Pain of Reverse Parallel Parking

It's Christmas Eve and you have to do your Christmas shopping. The shopping-centre car park is full and the only space you can find nearby is small and requires you to reverse parallel park. Do you attempt to park there, or try to find somewhere else? According to research, most women would prefer to park the car in a larger space somewhere else and walk back to their destination rather than reverse park into a tight spot.

> *Most women rate parking at Christmas on a par with a gynaecological examination.*

If you were asked to look at cars that had been reverse parked in that street, could you tell which cars had been parked by men and which by women? Research commissioned by an English defensive driving school showed that men in the UK averaged 82 per cent accuracy in reverse parking someone else's car close to the kerb and 71 per cent could successfully park their vehicle on the first attempt. Women scored only 22 per cent accuracy, while a mere 23 per cent could do it successfully on the first attempt. A similar study in Singapore gave men an accuracy score of 66 per cent, with 68 per cent doing it first time. For women, the accuracy result was 19 per cent, and only 12 per cent did it the first time. The bottom line: if the driver is a Singaporean woman, get out of the way!

Parking tests at driving schools show that women generally do better at reverse parking than men during driver training, but statistics show women perform worse in real-life situations. This is because women are better than men at learning a task and successfully repeating it, provided the environment and conditions under which they do it don't change. In traffic, however, every situation presents a new set of data to be assessed and men's spatial ability is better suited to handle this task.

Our hormones have a huge impact on our spatial ability. While testosterone will improve spatial ability, the female hormone, oestrogen, suppresses it. Women have dramatically less testosterone than men and, as a result, the more feminine the brain, the less the spatial ability. There is a rare condition known as Turner's syndrome where a genetic female (XX) is missing one of the X chromosomes and she is known as an XO girl. These girls are super-feminine in all their behaviours and have little or no directional or spatial ability. Never lend your car keys to an XO woman.

In recent times many regional towns and cities have introduced 45-degree rear-to-kerb reverse parking because it has been shown to be safer by allowing the driver to drive forward when they depart. Unfortunately, this has not helped most women's concerns about reverse parking as it still requires spatial abilities to estimate angles and distances. We surveyed 20 local councils who implemented this type of reverse parking and discovered that there were practically no women involved in the decision. It was almost always men. If a council was made up completely of women, reverse and parallel parking would no longer be allowed! They would arrange for drive-through-style parking that eliminates the need for reversing or estimating angles and distances. This would take up a greater amount of space, but there would be fewer accidents. It would also mean that women could get their Christmas shopping done more quickly as they'd be able to park nearer the shopping centre. It wouldn't make much difference to men – they'd probably still leave their shopping until 4.30 p.m. on Christmas Eve.

Can You Improve Your Spatial Skill?

In a word, yes. There are several alternatives. You can wait for the natural process of evolution to take place and constantly

practise your spatial activities until your brain develops suffi-
cient connections. Be prepared for the long haul with this
one, though. You certainly won't be able to do it in time for
next Christmas. Biologists estimate that it could take thousands of years.

*If you start now, you might be able to improve your
spatial skills in time for Christmas in the year 4000!*

A course of testosterone hormones will also improve spatial
ability, but this is not a satisfactory option as the downside
includes increased aggression level and baldness, which might
not suit most women. It can also give you a beard. No woman
wants to look like Father Christmas.

It is now clear that practice and repetition help perman-
ently to create more brain connections for a given task. Rats
raised in cages full of toys have more brain mass than rats
with no toys. Humans who retire to do nothing lose their
brain mass, whereas those who keep active mental interests
maintain mass and even increase it. Learning and practising
how maps work can greatly increase your practical ability to
use them, just as daily practice on the piano makes for more
competent playing. Unless the player has the kind of brain
circuitry that facilitates intuitive playing, however, lots of regular practice is required to maintain a reasonable level. Unless
the piano player or map reader keeps that up, their skill level
will diminish more quickly and take longer to recover than a
person whose brain is wired to handle the task.

*Poor map reading and getting lost account for 56 per cent
of arguments in cars. That's why Father Christmas doesn't
take his wife with him when he's delivering presents.*

Problem 2 – How a Car Drive Nearly Ruined Christmas Day

Don't worry – we're not going to let men get off too lightly! It's the next day, Christmas morning, and John and Ruth are now on their way to visit Ruth's parents, who have just moved into their brand-new home. John and Ruth haven't been to this part of town before and they haven't bought their street directory, but John is convinced he knows the way. Ruth thinks they are hopelessly lost, but now John is certain that he can find it. Ruth tentatively turns to John.

'Darling, I think we should have turned right at the traffic lights. Let's stop and ask directions.'

'There's no problem. I know it's around here somewhere . . .'

'But we've been trying to find it for ages – let's just stop and ask someone!'

'Listen, I know what I'm doing! Do you want to drive, or are you going to let me?'

'No, I don't want to drive, but I don't want to spend Christmas going round and round in circles either!'

'OK, then, why don't we turn the car round and we'll go back home!'

✳

Most men and women will recognise this conversation. A woman can't understand why this wonderful man she loves so much suddenly turns into Mad Max on steroids just because he's lost. If she was lost, she'd ask for directions, so what's his problem? Why can't he just admit he doesn't know?

....

Why did the Three Wise Men miss the birth of Jesus?
They refused to ask for directions.

....

Why Won't Men Stop and Ask for Directions?

Because they hate to be wrong. To understand why men hate to be wrong, it's important to understand the history of where this attitude came from. Picture this scene. The cave family is crouched around a fire. The man is sitting at the cave entrance gazing out, surveying the landscape and scanning the horizon for signs of movement. The woman and children have not eaten for days and he knows that he must hunt at the first break in the weather and not return until he has found food. This is his role and his family are depending on him. They're hungry but confident he can succeed as he has always done. His stomach is churning and he is fearful. Will he be successful again? Will his family starve? Will other males kill him because he is weak from hunger? He just sits there with a blank, expressionless face – watching. He must not show any signs of fear to his family as they would become disheartened. He must be strong.

In being wrong, a man considers himself a failure because he has not been able to do his job properly.

Why does it take 4 million male sperm
to find and fertilise an egg?
Not one wants to ask for directions.

It may be Christmas, but that's no reason to change a million years of not wanting to be seen as a failure. Most women don't know that if a man is driving in the car alone, he'd probably stop and ask directions. But to do it when she is in the car makes him feel like he is a failure because he couldn't get her there.

Christmas comes but once a year –
so why change a habit of a million years?

When a woman says, 'Let's ask directions,' a man hears, 'You're incompetent, you can't navigate.' If she says, 'The kitchen tap is leaking, let's call a plumber,' he hears, 'You're useless, I'll get another man to do it!' This is also the reason men have difficulty saying, 'I'm sorry.' They see it as admitting they are wrong, and to be wrong is to fail.

To deal with this problem, a woman needs to make sure that she doesn't make a man feel wrong when she discusses problems with him. Even giving a man a self-help book for Christmas is often interpreted by him as, 'You're not good enough.'

Men hate criticism –
that's why they like to marry virgins.

A man needs to understand that a woman's objective is not to make him wrong; it's to help him and he should not take things personally. A woman wants to improve the man she loves, but he interprets this as meaning that he is not good enough. A man won't admit mistakes because he thinks she won't love him. But the reality is, a woman loves a man more when he will admit mistakes.

A man would rather spend Christmas driving in circles
and saying, 'I'm sure it's around here somewhere,' and,
'I'm in the general area,' than admit he's wrong.

A quick, safe emergency strategy is to tell him you urgently need to go to the toilet, which will force him to stop, and preferably at a service station. While you're in the toilet, he'll have time to pretend he's buying something and to ask for directions. That way, you'll make it to your relatives' house in time for Christmas.

....

*'What's with you men? Would hair stop growing
on your chest if you asked directions somewhere?'*
ERMA BOMBECK

....

The Flying Map

We (the authors) travel the world for nine months of the year giving seminars, and spend much of our time in hire cars. Like most people, we also have to spend a considerable amount of time driving between relatives and friends at Christmas. Allan normally drives as his spatial skills are better than Barbara's, which leaves her to navigate. Barbara has almost no navigational ability so she and Allan have argued and fought their way around the world and across the country for years. Allan has had street directories and maps thrown at him in practically every language by Barbara, and on several occasions she has fled from him and his maps, catching buses or trains and shouting, 'Read it yourself!' There have been one or two abandoned Christmas parties as well.

....

*Barbara has no sense of direction,
but Allan can never find socks in his drawer.*

....

Fortunately, their research into spatial ability alerted them to the problems that arise when one partner has little spatial ability and the other does not understand this. Today, Allan reads the map before driving and Barbara talks and points out interesting features of the landscape that Allan normally misses. They are still happily married, flying maps no longer pose a hazard to passing motorists, and arguments haven't ruined Christmas in a long, long time.

Summary: How to Avoid an Argument While Driving This Christmas

John and Ruth now get on well when they travel together. For Christmas this year, Ruth bought him a hand-held satellite navigation system. This means that he can decide which route they will take and he navigates. A GPS is an excellent spatial 'boys' toy' that will allow him always to be right, never be lost and to love you for ever. If a GPS is out of your price range but he likes computers, there are now CD-ROMs available for most major cities that plot the perfect route, which you can print out and take on any Christmas journey.

While John is driving and navigating, Ruth talks and points out landmarks and he listens, without interruption. She no longer criticises his driving because she knows that his spatial ability lets him take what she may consider a risk, but to him is perfectly safe driving.

When men stop asking women to navigate, everyone's lives will be happier, and when women stop criticising men's driving ability and asking them to stop for directions, there will be far fewer arguments at Christmas. We are all good at different things so if you are not good at a particular task, don't worry about it. You can improve with practice, but don't let it ruin your life or your Christmas.

Chapter 5

TEN THINGS MEN AND WOMEN DO AT CHRISTMAS THAT ANNOY EACH OTHER

The story of the Three Wise Men and the birth of Christ is one of the world's most told tales. It's also one that, for women, illustrates all of the male species' traits that frustrate them. First of all, they simply assumed the heavens revolved around them – the star shining in the East had been put there expressly for them to follow. Secondly, they didn't arrive at the stable where Jesus was born until more than two months after the event, most probably because they refused to stop on the way and ask for directions. Thirdly, what possible use would a new-born baby and his exhausted new mother want with gifts of gold, frankincense (a resin used for fumigation) and myrrh (a strong-smelling plant oil used for embalming the dead)? And, finally, Three Wise Men? Who's ever seen such an unlikely sight?

Imagine if the story had starred Three Wise Women. They would have asked directions, arrived in time to help deliver the baby and brought practical gifts, like nappies, bottles, toys and a bouquet of flowers. They would then have put the animals outside, cleaned the stables, made a casserole, stayed in touch by mail, and there would be peace on Earth for ever more.

Having said that, if there had been Three Wise Women, they might have missed Christmas altogether because they all went off to the toilet on Christmas Eve and got talking.

❋

For over a decade, we have collected and recorded responses to surveys about the things men and women do that most frustrate each other, and we have drawn on the science of human behaviour to explain their differences. Most importantly, we have developed strategies for dealing with these differences. When it comes to Christmas, the list of things that men and women do that annoy each other is surprisingly long, but we've whittled it down and come up with the ten questions men and women most frequently ask about each other during the festive season. Here are the questions:

1 Why do men spend all Christmas playing computer games?
2 Why can men never find sellotape, scissors and anything else they need at Christmas?
3 Why can women never put the Christmas tree up straight?
4 Why do men like playing those annoying puzzles that come in Christmas crackers?
5 Why do men keep flicking through the channels with the remote control?
6 Why do men insist on leaving the toilet seat up, even when your parents are staying?
7 Why do women always go to the toilet with other women at parties?
8 Why do men love gross jokes?
9 Why can women never manage to record the one thing you want to watch at Christmas?
10 Why do some men complain of being bored over Christmas?

1 Why Do Men Spend All Christmas Playing Computer Games?

We are often asked why men spend so much time glued to the PlayStation or X-Box over Christmas, while women seem to have little or no interest. The answer is simple: computer and console games require men to use their spatial skills.

Visit any video or pinball arcade in the world and you'll see that it's full of teenage boys using their spatial skills. Go to any shop selling computer games and you'll notice that it's packed with men. Let's look at some of the scientific studies highlighting spatial ability. Most of them involved the assembly of three-dimensional mechanical apparatus.

Yale University carried out a study that revealed only 22 per cent of females could perform such tasks as well as males. Boys excelled when their right eye was covered so that only the left eye could receive information that was fed to the right brain, where most spatial skills are located. It made no difference to girls which eye they used, because their brain tried to solve the problems using both sides. This is why women rarely choose to be motor mechanics, engineers or airline pilots.

Iowa State University professor of psychology Dr Camilla Benbow and colleague Dr Julian Stanley tested a group of gifted children and found that boys who were good at maths outnumbered girls by 13:1. Boys can construct a block building from two-dimensional plans more easily and quickly than girls; they can estimate angles accurately and can see whether a flat surface is level. On three-dimensional video tests, boys outstripped girls in spatial ability by a ratio of 4:1, and the best girls were often outclassed by the lowest-scoring boys. With males, this is a specific brain function located in at least four sites in the right front hemisphere and several smaller areas in the left. Dr Benbow also reported that differences between the sexes in terms of spatial ability were already striking by the age of four.

These ancient hunting skills are the reason men dominate areas like architecture, chemistry, building and statistics. Boys test better in hand-eye coordination, making them more proficient at ball sports. This accounts for the male obsession with any game that involves estimating coordinates and throwing, chasing or shooting at a target. It also explains why video and pinball arcades and skateboard rinks around the world are full of boys but there are few girls. Most of the girls are there to impress the boys, but, as most teenage girls quickly learn, the boys are more obsessed with the games than they are in noticing them.

....

Men like to play computer games at Christmas because they test their spatial skills, not because they want to get out of cooking Christmas dinner.

....

Computer games are a particular problem at Christmas because games and consoles are often given as presents to men and boys – leading to countless festive hours spent sitting in front of it, and just as many trying to make them hear you when you ask them to stop! If a woman doesn't wish her partner to play computer games over Christmas, she should talk to him about it *before* Christmas and suggest that he doesn't play on Christmas Day or that he perhaps only plays for an hour at most. If he doesn't listen, you may be forced to remove the games console for the day. If a woman has bought her partner a computer game for Christmas, she has to expect that he will want to play it.

2   Why Can Men Never Find Sellotape, Scissors and Anything Else They Need at Christmas?

Every woman in the world has had the following conversation with a male who is standing in front of an open fridge:

DAVID: 'Where's the butter?'
JAN: 'It's in the fridge.'
DAVID: 'I'm looking there, but I can't see any butter.'
JAN: 'Well, it's there. I put it in ten minutes ago!'

DAVID: 'No. You must have moved it. There's definitely no butter in this fridge!'

At that, Jan strides into the kitchen, thrusts her arm into the fridge and, as if by magic, produces a tub of butter. Inexperienced men sometimes feel that this is a trick and they accuse women of always hiding things from them in drawers and cupboards.

At Christmas, the list of things that men 'can't find' is seemingly endless – when wrapping presents (yes, some men do!), they can't find the sellotape, or the scissors, or the ribbon, and, now they think about it, they're not really sure where the presents have got to either. They're all there, they just can't see them. Men don't just say this to cause a festive feud – there is a scientific reason why men can't find things.

Eyes in the Back of Her Head?

Well, not quite, but close. Women have wider peripheral vision than men. As a nest-defender, a woman has brain software that allows her to receive an arc of at least 45 degrees clear vision to each side of her head and above and below her nose. Many women's peripheral vision is effective up to almost 180 degrees. A man's eyes are larger than a woman's and his brain configures them for a type of long-distance tunnel vision, which means that he can see clearly and accurately directly in front of him and over greater distances, almost like a pair of binoculars.

With her wider arc of peripheral vision, a woman can see most of the contents of a cupboard or a fridge without moving her head. This is why she finds it easier to locate things like scissors in a drawer or butter in the fridge. Her oestrogen hormones allow her to identify matching items in a drawer, cupboard or across a room and later remember objects in a complex random pattern – such as where the ribbon is in relation to the sellotape in the cupboard. New research also suggests that male brains are searching for the word to go with the item, so, in the case of the butter, he's looking for B-U-T-T-E-R. If it's facing the wrong way, he virtually can't see it. This is why men move their heads. Men move their heads from side to side and up and down as they scan for the 'missing' objects.

....

*Men's tunnel vision explains why men constantly
have to ask women where things are at Christmas.*

....

As a hunter, a man needed vision that would allow him to zero in on, and pursue, targets in the distance. He evolved with almost blinkered vision so that he would not be distracted from targets, whereas a woman needed eyes to allow a wide arc of vision so that she could monitor any predators sneaking up on the nest.

You can increase your peripheral vision range with practice, just as fighter pilots do, but it takes a while, so don't count on being able to do it in time for Christmas. The arc of a person's peripheral vision can also increase under life-threatening circumstances. During a prison riot at Australia's Perth Prison in 1999, inmates held several prison officers hostage. They announced that unless their demands were met, the officers would be killed. Prison officer Lance Bremen reported that, until that time, he had 'typical male tunnel vision'. Having survived the incident, his peripheral vision had increased to almost 180 degrees. Because of the trauma of the event and the fear of being killed, his brain had expanded his vision range to monitor anyone trying to sneak up on him.

A woman's Christmas is much less stressful when she understands the problems men have seeing things at close range. When he's trying to wrap a present and he says, 'Honey, where's the sellotape? Have you seen the ribbon? Where have you put the scissors? I think we must be out of gift tags . . .' a woman should just accept that it's harder for him to see them than it is her. And when a woman tells a man, 'It's in the cupboard!' it is less stressful for him to believe her and continue the search. This is definitely the best route to a peaceful Christmas.

3   Why Can Women Never Put the Christmas Tree Up Straight?

We are all familiar with the agony of trying to get the Christmas tree straight in its holder. Across the world, there are people asking, 'Is it straight yet?' Putting up a Christmas tree is definitely a two-person job, but we suggest that the man is the one to adjust its position if you want to make sure it is at a 90-degree angle.

As we have seen, women generally have better peripheral vision than men and are better at seeing fine detail, but it's a fact that they will be more likely to struggle to tell whether the Christmas tree is straight. One of our friends said he couldn't believe how wonderful his wife's eyesight was when he had something to hide, but how it seemed to desert her totally when it came to backing the car into the garage. Putting up a Christmas tree, like estimating the distance between the car bumper and the garage wall while moving, is a spatial skill located in the right hemisphere in men and is not strong in most women.

Getting the tree straight is all about angles, and angles are male heaven. A man finds it easy to visualise in his head what the effect will be of tilting the tree slightly to the left, while women invariably tilt it the wrong way or move it too far. The male brain is expert at estimating speeds, angles and direction. This is why men like ball games so much, which are also all about predicting angles and direction.

The same is true for buying a Christmas tree – take the story of Carol and her tree. For years Carol had bought trees that were either too tall or too small for the room. Eventually, she gave up on estimating which tree would look right and simply measured the height of the room and then took the tape measure with her so that she could measure the height of the tree to make sure it would fit. One year, however, her 15-year-old son, Michael, went to buy the Christmas tree. Carol told him to measure the height of the room and to take the tape measure with him. He said, 'Don't worry – I don't need it.' Carol couldn't understand how Michael could know this. When he returned with the tree, it fitted the space exactly. She could not comprehend how he could look at a tree and imagine whether or not it would fit into the house. And how did he do it? He used his spatial ability.

4 Why Do Men Like Playing Those Annoying Puzzles That Come in Christmas Crackers?

Puzzles that come in Christmas crackers – such as the classic maze puzzle – are notoriously frustrating and take hours to complete. Plus, they require a more steady hand than most of us have after a few glasses of wine on Christmas Day. However, many men seem to love them and can often spend a Christmas afternoon hunched over one, trying to nudge the tiny ball-bearings to the centre of the maze. Some women might argue that men like to play Christmas-cracker puzzles because it gets them out of doing the washing-up after Chrismas dinner, but in fact there is a biological explanation.

American scientist Dr D. Wechsler created a series of IQ tests that eliminated sexual bias against men or women during spatial tests. By testing members of cultures from primitive races to sophisticated city dwellers all over the world, he, like other researchers elsewhere, came to the conclusion that women had superiority over men in general intelligence, being around 3 per cent more intelligent than men, despite having slightly smaller brains. When it came to solving maze puzzles, however, men were overwhelmingly superior to women, scoring 92 per cent of the top honours against women's 8 per cent, regardless of culture. Critics might say this proves women are too intelligent to play silly maze puzzles, but it does graphically demonstrate male spatial ability.

Tests by zoologists show that male mammals are superior to female mammals in spatial abilities – male rats are far better at finding their way out of mazes than female rats, and male elephants are better than females at relocating a water-hole.

Maze puzzles, mini pinball puzzles, ball-bearing puzzles, mini Rubik's Cubes and other games that you find in Christmas crackers all test your brain's ability to rotate a three-dimensional object using angles and imagine the outcome. It requires your brain to make spatial rotations, which explains why men enjoy them and are better at them than women. It doesn't explain why nobody has come up with a Christmas-cracker gift that women will enjoy, however – miniature sewing kits and plastic rings just don't come close.

5 Why Do Men Keep Flicking Through the Channels With the Remote Control?

> **Remote control:** (noun, female) a device for changing one TV channel to another; (noun, male) a device for scanning through 55 channels every 2.5 minutes.

You've made it – the presents are unwrapped, Christmas dinner is over for another year, the dishes are done, the kids seem happy. All that's left to do is snuggle down on the sofa with a glass of hot mulled wine and watch that Christmas movie première you've been looking forward to all week. Unfortunately, your definition of *watching* is not the same as your partner's. Just as you sit down, he flicks channels. A minute later he flicks again. And again. Finally, you crack: 'I just want to watch TV.'

He turns to you, completely at a loss as to why you have lost your temper. 'But we are watching TV,' he says.

At Christmas, men don't want to know what's on television; they want to know what else is on television.

For thousands of years, men would return from the hunt at the end of the day and spend the evening just gazing into the fire. A man would sit in this trance-like state among his friends for long periods without communicating, and the other men made no demands on him to speak or participate. For men, this was a valuable form of stress relief and a way to recharge their batteries for the next day's activities. For modern men, fire-gazing still occurs, but now involves tools like newspapers, books and remote controls.

Once, we were at the remote Okavango Delta, north of Botswana's Kalahari Desert in southern Africa. Noticing a satellite dish powered by a solar cell on a pole above a village hut, we went inside and found a group of Kalahari bushmen dressed in loincloths in front of a television set with a remote control, each taking turns to flick through all the channels.

Christmas is a time of tradition ... the traditional fight over the remote control, the traditional complaints that there is nothing good on TV ...

Male channel-changing is a pet hate of women everywhere. It's a common joke that many would like to bury their husbands with the remote control firmly clasped in their hand. And at Christmas, at the end of a long day of eating, drinking and more eating, this is never more of a problem.

Television channels are vying for your attention and consequently at peak times there can be a range of programmes that you'd like to watch on at the same time. This makes men's channel-surfing worse than ever.

It doesn't help matters that women and men's tastes in television programmes differs so much. A woman likes to relax by becoming involved in a television show, especially a film involving human interaction and emotional scenes, so at Christmas she'll probably want to watch a romantic comedy, an emotional drama or a costume drama. Her brain is organised to read the words and body language of the actors and she likes to predict outcomes of relationship scenarios. For men, however, watching television is a completely different process, done to satisfy two main impulses. Firstly, having a solution-oriented, problem-solving brain, he is interested in getting to the bottom line as quickly as possible. By flicking through the channels, he can analyse the problems in each programme and consider the solutions needed. Secondly, men like to forget about their own problems by looking at someone else's, which explains why six times as many men watch the TV evening news bulletins as women. Since his mind can only do one thing at a time, by looking at other people's problems and not feeling responsible for them, he can forget about his own worries. At Christmas, he'll probably want to watch an action film or a thriller (preferably both at the same time). This basic difference between the sexes frequently leads to trouble.

How do you get a man to burn off
some Christmas calories?
Put the remote control between his toes.

To solve the remote-control problem, a woman needs to calmly discuss with him how much it drives her crazy, and could he please not do it when she is watching her programme, and especially not do it at Christmas. Alternatively, she can try hiding the remote somewhere he'd never think of looking. And if neither of those work, she should consider asking for her own television set for Christmas – or another remote control.

6   Why Do Men Insist on Leaving the Toilet Seat Up, Even When Your Parents Are Staying?

Jill has got her parents round for Christmas for the first time. The house is spotless, Christmas dinner was a huge success – everything is going well. There's just one small thing . . . her husband, Bob, keeps leaving the toilet seat up. She's been through this with him a million times but he keeps doing it. Jill keeps running in there to put it down every time he goes to the toilet so her mother doesn't see. Why can't he just put it down afterwards?

In order to understand this most frustrating of male habits, we need to look back to history . . .

Until the end of the late 1800s, when the flushing toilet was invented, toilets were small boxes out the back of a home. Whenever a woman was going to use the toilet, she would take other women with her for security. Men, however, were expected to go alone and defend themselves if necessary. Men never peed in the toilet – they did it in a bush or up against something, a habit that modern men have inherited from their forefathers. This is why you rarely see a man peeing in an open field, it's always up against something like a wall or a tree, and, just like other animals, there's an intrinsic element of marking one's territory.

Today, public toilets everywhere have separate-sex toilet facilities, with seats for women and wall-mounted urinals for men. Women always sit down, but men only sit 10 to 20 per cent of the time. Modern homes are supposedly designed and built to accommodate both men and women equally, but men are disadvantaged in that home toilets only accommodate women's needs. In the home, a man will lift the seat so as not to wet it for a woman, who will sit on it. But when he fails to put it down afterwards, he's roundly criticised. Many men resent that a great deal. Why shouldn't women take a turn in putting the seat up for men?

....

When God had finished creating the Universe he realised he had two things left over to divide between Adam and Eve. One, he explained, was an implement that would allow its owner to pee standing up. Adam was thrilled, and begged and begged that he be allowed to have it.

Eve smiled graciously and told God that if Adam really wanted it so badly, he should have it. So God gave it to Adam, who immediately went off and excitedly peed up against a tree, and drew a pattern in the sand. And God saw that it was good.

God then turned to Eve. 'Well, here's the other thing,' he said. 'I guess you can have it.'

'Thanks,' replied Eve. 'What's it called?'

God smiled back as he answered, 'Multiple orgasms.'

....

In Sweden a few years ago, a feminist group called for men's urinals to be banned on the grounds that men standing up to pee were 'triumphing in their masculinity' and thus degrading women. They didn't win too much support. In some places, usually trendy advertising offices in the USA, urinals are increasingly being phased out, however, in preference for unisex toilets, all with their individual cubicles, although more on the grounds of saving money and optimising space than any arguments about the equality of the sexes. A Dutch company in the year 2000 announced the launch on to the market of the world's first 'female urinal'. So far, they haven't made a huge impact on global toilet habits.

One of our male readers wrote to us about how he and his wife tackled the ongoing toilet-seat argument:

Women should understand that sometimes a man's penis has a mind of its own. A man can go into a toilet cubicle (because all the urinals are being used), take perfect aim at the toilet, and his penis will still manage to pee all over the roll of toilet paper, down his left pant leg and on to his shoe. I'm telling you, John Thomas can't be trusted.

After being married 28 years, my wife has now trained me. I'm no longer allowed to pee like a man – standing up. I'm required to sit down and pee. She has convinced me that this is a small price to pay. Otherwise, if she goes to the toilet one more time at night and either sits on a pee-soaked toilet seat or falls into the toilet because I didn't put the seat down, she's going to murder me in my sleep.

There's also the problem of the morning erection, which makes it doubly difficult for a man to have a true aim, and explains how the wallpaper gets wet. Even sitting down, he reported, there are major mechanical problems that only men understand. He's now perfected the art of lying face down over the toilet bowl in a 'Flying Superman' position in order to make sure that nothing escapes.

Women need to understand that men are not totally to blame. We are sensitive to their concerns about hygiene and bathroom cleanliness, but there are times when things just get beyond our control. It's not our fault, it's Mother Nature. If it was Father Nature . . . there wouldn't have been a problem.

In truth, men don't really care about whether the seat is up or down, but can get annoyed with a woman who demands it is lowered, rather than asking him politely – or doing it herself. So what should Jill do about Bob? Asking a man to sit down when he pees will usually mean no more problems. If the man refuses, it should be quietly, but firmly, pointed out that many hundreds of thousands of men in the Muslim world sit down to pee every day – without feeling their masculinity is in the slightest bit compromised. The Prophet was said to only have urinated once standing, and that was when he was in a garden where it was impossible to sit down. If that fails to persuade a man, simply set new house rules. From now on it's his job to clean the toilet, and that means mopping the floor every day to clear up all the stray droplets. That might very soon put a whole new positive light on the seated position . . .

If you can afford it, the ideal solution is always to buy a home with two toilets – one for him and one for her – or renovate a current home to include an extra bathroom. That way, you can both enjoy the standards of cleanliness and hygiene you choose, without having to feel stressed about the other's, and it won't pose a problem when guests come to stay at Christmas.

7 Why Do Women Always Go to the Toilet With Other Women at Parties?

At Christmas, we socialise more than at any other time of the year. Unfortunately, this means that husbands are often left standing around at parties wondering where their wives have got to. Why do women go to the toilet in groups, and why do they spend so long in there?

As we learned earlier, the flushing toilet wasn't invented until the early nineteenth century. Up until then, men and women would have to venture down to the back of the home to use the toilet. Men would go alone, but whenever a woman was going to use the toilet, she would take other women with her for security. When the flushing toilet was invented (purportedly by Thomas Crapper), the humble loo moved to its own room inside houses and public establishments, yet the practice of going to the toilet in groups still persists for women. A man will never be heard to say, 'Hey, Fred, I'm going to the toilet . . . would you like to come?'

When women go to the bathroom, they take a support group.

When women go to the toilet together, they talk – it is a chance to bond and form closer relationships with other women. When men go to the restroom together, they don't talk. Even if he's in there with his best friend, talk is still kept to a minimum. And a man never talks to another strange man in a public toilet. Never, ever, under any circumstances. Here's a letter from one of our male readers, demonstrating the point about the kind of hush reigning in the men's restroom:

I was driving north on the motorway when I pulled in at a rest stop to use the men's room. The first cubicle was occupied so I went into the second. I was barely sitting down when a voice from the other cubicle said, 'Hi, how are you?'

Like all men, I never start a conversation with a stranger or fraternise in men's rooms at a rest stop, and I still don't know what got into me, but I answered with an embarrassed 'Not bad!'

The other guy said, 'So . . . what are you up to?'

I was thinking, 'This is bizarre,' but, like a fool, I answered, 'Same as you . . . just travelling north!'

Then I heard the guy say nervously, 'Listen . . . I'll have to call you back, there's an idiot in the other stall who keeps answering my questions!'

Unlike men, when women go to the toilet, they talk about everything and everybody. They talk about what they're doing for Christmas and New Year's, they discuss clothing they and others are wearing – 'Did you see that woman in the purple dress? I'd never be caught dead in that!' – who the nice men are, who they don't like, and any personal problems they or their friends may be having. When fixing their make-up, they'll discuss application techniques and different types of products, and will share cosmetics with others, including strangers. Any woman who looks upset is given group therapy . . . and heaven help the man who upset her! Women will sit on the toilet and talk to other women through the wall, they will ask strangers to pass toilet paper under the gap, and it's not unknown for two women to use the same cubicle so they can continue their conversation. One nightclub in Birmingham, England, has even installed extra-large cubicles in the ladies' restroom and each has two toilets for deep and meaningful conversations. At Christmas, practically the whole female contingent of the party decamps to the ladies' bathroom!

> *The real Christmas party is the one going on in the ladies' restroom.*

8   Why Do Men Love Gross Jokes?

Christmas is a time of laughter and frivolity. It's a time to indulge our pleasures and share a joke with friends and family. The trouble is, men tend to crack jokes about sex or horrific events. This usually doesn't pose a problem when you are with your friends, who are likely to share a similar sense of humour. But, at Christmas, when you may have family and elderly relatives round, and even children, this can be a little awkward. So why do men insist on telling disgusting jokes?

The main purpose of humour for men is threefold: first, to gain status with other men by having a good repertoire; second, to allow him to deal with tragic events or consequences;

third, to acknowledge the truth about a topical issue. This is why almost all jokes have a punchline, which is usually a disastrous ending. Laughter is rooted in our ancient past, where it was used as a warning signal to tell other humans that there was imminent danger, just like it's used in the ape family. If, for example, a chimpanzee narrowly escapes being attacked by a lion, it will scamper up a tree, throw its head back and make a series of HOO-HOO-HOO-HAR-HAR-HAR sounds that resemble human laughter. This warns other chimps about the danger. Laughing is an extension of crying, and crying is a startled fear reaction, which is evident in infants from birth. If you intentionally frighten a child by playing peek-a-boo, its first response is to cry out of fear. When the child realises the situation is not life-threatening, it will laugh, signifying that while it experienced a fear reaction, the laughter signals it now knows it was only a trick.

Brain scans show that men laugh more at things that stimulate the right brain than the left, but for women it's the opposite. In America, Rochester University claims to have found where the male sense of humour comes from – it's located in the right frontal lobe of the brain above the right eye. Men love humour or any joke that has a logical, step-by-step approach with a conclusion that is hard to predict. Here are a couple of tame Christmas jokes that stimulate male brains:

....

What's the difference between snowmen and snowladies?
Snowballs.

....

Why is Christmas just like a day at the office?
You do all the work and the fat guy in the suit
gets all the credit.

....

A major difference between the sexes is men's obsession with telling jokes about tragedies, horrific events and male genitalia.

Women's sex organs can perform astounding feats of human reproduction, are securely hidden away and if unravelled, would stretch over 4 kilometres. But women never make jokes about them, give them pet names or treat them as a source of laughter.

Men's sex organs hang out the front in a vulnerable and precarious position (further proof that God is female) and are a constant source of male amusement and hilarity. Women's humour involves people, relationships and men. For example:

....

How do you know Santa is a woman?
Because men never pack their own bag, they
don't answer their mail, they're not interested in
stockings unless someone's wearing them, and
being responsible for Christmas would require
a commitment.

....

Male brains have an amazing capacity for remembering and storing jokes. Some men can tell jokes they heard in fourth grade but don't know the names of their children's best friends. Males think it is hilarious to moon (give a 'brown eye') from a moving car to an unsuspecting group of elderly ladies, especially nuns, put superglue or cling film on a toilet seat, hold a farting competition or chain a drunken, naked groom-to-be to a lamppost. To most women, none of these things is remotely funny.

Jokes are so important as a communication medium to men that whenever there is a global tragedy, the world's email networks and faxes are literally swamped with men sending tragedy-related jokes. Whether it's the death of Princess Diana, September 11 or the hunt for Osama bin Laden, the male brain instantly swings into action.

*Osama bin Laden has 53 brothers and sisters,
13 wives, 28 children and is worth over $300 million.
But he hates Americans because of their excessive
lifestyles.*

Herein lies the difference between men and women in handling serious emotional issues. Women deal with calamity or tragedy by openly expressing their emotions to others, but men withhold their emotions. Men use joke-telling as their way of 'talking' about the event without showing any strong emotions that could be seen as a weakness.

How Jokes and Humour Ease Pain

Laughing and crying instruct the brain to release endorphins into the bloodstream. An endorphin is a chemical that has a similar composition to morphine and heroin, and has a tranquillising effect on the body while, at the same time, building the immune system. This explains why happy people rarely get sick, and miserable people who complain a lot often seem to fall ill.

Laughter and crying are closely linked from a psychological and physiological standpoint. Think of the last time someone told you a joke that made you buckle up with uncontrollable laughter. How did you feel afterwards? That tingling sensation came from your brain releasing endorphins into your blood system, giving a natural 'high'. In effect, you were 'stoned'. Those who have trouble with laughing at life often turn to drugs, alcohol or sex to achieve that same feeling. Alcohol loosens inhibitions and lets people laugh, releasing endorphins, which is why most well-adjusted people laugh more when they drink alcohol and unhappy people become even more miserable or even violent.

'The Supreme Court has ruled that they cannot have a nativity scene in Washington, DC. This wasn't for any religious reasons. They couldn't find three wise men and a virgin.'

JAY LENO

At the end of a big laughing session, you will often cry. 'I just laughed until I cried!' Tears contain encephalin, which is another of the body's natural tranquillisers to relieve pain. We cry when we experience a painful event, and endorphins and encephalin aid in self-anaesthesia.

The basis of many jokes is that something disastrous or painful happens to a person. But because we know that it is not a real event happening, we laugh and release endorphins for self-anaesthesia. If it were a real event, we would go immediately into crying mode and the body would also release encephalin. This is why crying is often the extension of a laughing bout and why when faced with a serious emotional crisis such as a death, many people cry, but a person who cannot mentally accept the death may begin laughing. When reality hits, the laughter turns to tears.

Laughter anaesthetises the body, builds the immune system, defends against illness and disease, aids memory, teaches more efficiently and extends life. Humour heals. Research around the world has now shown how the positive effects of laughing, with the release of the body's own painkillers, strengthen the immune system. After laughter, the pulse rate steadies, breathing deepens, arteries dilate and the muscles relax.

This is a predominantly male way of dealing with emotional pain. The harder it is for a man to talk about an emotional event, the harder he will laugh when told a joke about it, however heartless and insensitive it may seem to women. Men rarely talk about their sex lives to other men so they tell jokes about it as a way of discussing it. Women, however, will discuss their sex lives with their girlfriends in graphic detail without the aid of any jokes.

Don't Let It Ruin Your Christmas

As long as there are Irish men, there will be Irish jokes. Or Asian or Aussie or feminist jokes. And every time there's a tragedy, it will invariably spawn its own set of jokes.

Being offended is a choice. Others can't offend you – you choose to be offended. And choosing offence tells the world that you are unable to come to terms with the problem addressed by the joke. We are Australian authors living in England, and the English are always telling Australian jokes about us: 'What's the difference between Australia and yoghurt? At least yoghurt has some culture!', 'Why are Aussies so well balanced? Because they have a chip on both shoulders' and 'How can you tell a level-headed Australian? They dribble out of both sides of their mouth.'

With all these jokes, we don't choose to be offended. If it's a good joke, we'll laugh just as hard as the English. And later we might even adapt it to make it about Kiwis or Americans. Choosing offence is a negative choice, like shame, embarrassment or hurt. These choices may show others that you have low self-esteem, aren't in control of your own emotions or are not prepared to face a situation.

You can choose to feel offended because someone tells a joke that says anyone from your country is stupid. That doesn't mean they are stupid and even if you agree that they are, abusing the joke-teller won't make them any smarter. You can choose anger because the traffic is backed up, but it won't clear the traffic. If you take a calm, analytical approach about why the traffic is backed up, you may come up with a solution that can help solve the problem. There's no point in choosing anger.

If a man insists on telling inappropriate jokes at the wrong time or place, tell him you don't like it and you want him to stop. If he continues to do it, simply walk away and do something else.

At Christmas dinner, in front of your parents or grand-parents, that can be more difficult, particularly if you are the host. The man you're asking to stop telling inappropriate jokes may feel publicly humiliated, which may simply encourage him to tell even more outrageous jokes. It might be better to use the tactic of striking up a conversation about his jokes with the line 'Do you know any jokes that aren't nasty, or maybe all jokes are nasty?' That can then turn the dinner-table conversation to a general discussion about the nature of humour. You can always then dazzle your guests with your extensive knowledge of why men and women laugh at very different kinds of jokes!

9 Why Can Women Never Manage to Record the One Thing You Want to Watch at Christmas?

We are frequently asked this question as at Christmas there is lots on TV that you both want to watch. For instance, on Christmas Day, the man might agree to watch his partner's historical drama if she will record his action film for him. However, when he goes to watch it on Boxing Day, he discovers that she has set it to the wrong channel and accidentally recorded three hours of wildlife programmes. Why is this?

Essentially, it's once again down to the part of the brain called the visual-spatial area. It is used to measure speeds, angles, distances and spatial coordinates and is also the area used by modern males for such tasks as reverse parallel parking, merging on a motorway . . . and programming a video player. To put it in straightforward terms, it's the hunting part of the brain.

As we learned earlier, a study at Yale University found that only 22 per cent of females could perform such tasks as well as males. It also discovered that while 68 per cent of males could programme a VCR or similar equipment from a set of written instructions on the first attempt, only 16 per cent of females could do it.

If your partner is one of the 84 per cent that struggle with using the video recorder, we suggest that this Christmas you record anything you want to watch yourself, or buy another television!

10 Why Do Some Men Complain of Being Bored Over Christmas?

It's common knowledge that most men like to have something to do all the time – they fill their day with work, their evenings with TV and exercise, and their weekends with hobbies. Christmas can therefore be hard for some men – for a week, or perhaps even two, this is a work- and hobby-free zone. No sport, no computer games, no DIY projects, just quality time with family and friends. We are often asked by women why the thought of two weeks of not having to do things terrifies men so much and why they often become cranky and restless as a result. To understand this, let's look back to man's evolution.

Some men dread Christmas because the thought of not having to go to work and not knowing how to fill their time terrifies them.

For at least a hundred thousand years men have risen in the morning and gone out to find food for their families. A man's contribution to human survival was clear and simple – find an edible target and hit it. Consequently, the male brain evolved with specific areas to allow him successfully to do just that.

For tens of thousands of years, the male job description was specifically to hunt. Women evolved as nest-defenders –

their role was to ensure the survival of the next generation. Their brains evolved with different areas of strength to deal with that task – hitting a moving zebra at 30 metres was never part of that responsibility. This helps to explain why female brain scans show minimal activity in the spatial areas.

By the end of the eighteenth century, advanced farming techniques meant that hunting for food was no longer a priority. To deal with the frustration of no longer being required to chase and hit a target, men used two substitutes – work and sport. Both involve all the elements of hunting – stalking, chasing, aiming and hitting the target. Consequently, 90 per cent of all modern ball sports originated between AD 1800 and 1900 as a replacement for hunting. Again, this is why most men are obsessed with their work and sport, while most women are not.

Christmas poses a problem because suddenly they are no longer required to hit a moving target. And herein lies the problem for the modern man. He still has a highly configured hunting brain that is literally unemployed. He's all dressed up with nowhere to go.

So Why Don't Women Dread the Christmas Holidays?

Compared with men, most women tend to have no problem with not working over the Christmas holidays. Men have always defined themselves by their work and accomplishments; women usually judge their own self-worth by the quality of their relationships. Studies on male and female values continually show that 70 to 80 per cent of men everywhere say that the most important part of their lives is their work, and 70 to 80 per cent of women say the most important priority is their family.

A woman's identity is multi-faceted. She can be income-earner, carer, mother, grandmother, homemaker, socialiser, companion, wife and lover, at any given time, and often all at once. Christmas allows women to fulfil most of the roles they value, and, most importantly, it allows them to build relationships.

*Men value accomplishments, women value
relationships. This is why Christmas can be daunting
for men, while women see it as an opportunity.*

All of this also explains why retirement is so much harder for
men to handle than women. In fact, many men suffer a real
loss of identity when they retire; it is, in many ways, similar
to the death of a loved one and can even lead to depression.

The Christmas holidays can be difficult for couples. For
most of the year, one or both partners are at work all day and
they only see each other at weekends and evenings. Over the
holidays, however, they spend much more time together.
Female partners may see their husband, for the first time in
their lives, for breakfast, lunch and dinner. They can see he
has free time – but he still never offers to help with the housework. They don't understand why he is so restless. Consequently, resentment and anger can grow.

Men are used to the structure and routine of work. About
90 per cent of your day is made up of repetitive, organised
activity. When you are working, you don't have to consciously
decide to get out of bed at 6.30 a.m., drive to work and start
at 8 a.m.; you just do it every day. Your job may involve different problems, but, most of the time, your approach to
them will be the same as it has always been. Overall, your life
is a routine, and you feel confident and in control. When you
take time off, even for a period as short as Christmas, this
doesn't apply.

It is natural for men to want to keep busy over the holidays.
This is why many men take up DIY projects over Christmas.
Go to any DIY store between Christmas and New Year and
you'll see it's packed with men. Men want something to do to
keep them occupied, but they also want something to do that
makes them feel useful.

Chapter 6

'HOW LONG DID YOU SAY YOU WERE STAYING?'

You want to spend Christmas with the people you love and care about, but sometimes your relations can make Christmas hard work. According to one survey, over 2 million UK adults have ten or more relatives descending on their home for the festive celebrations. Blood may be thicker than water, but with so many different personalities, you will need thick skin to be able to deal with your family at Christmastime. The same survey revealed that 2 million Brits – possibly the same ones who have so many people coming to stay! – worry about relatives coming to visit for Christmas more than a month before they arrive.

....

'Christmas is a time when you get homesick –
even when you're home.'
CAROL NELSON

....

Guests staying too long, making a mess, being noisy and drinking too much are top of the list of reasons why having your family to stay for Christmas – or going to stay with them – can be stressful, and many couples report that family get-togethers often end in arguments and dissatisfaction. Plus, there's the annual debate over who is spending Christmas with whom, which, in today's world, is being made increasingly complicated by the rising incidences of divorce and separation. History can certainly play its part in making Christmas a battlefield, and if you're not careful, old grudges and long-forgotten disputes can rear their head. But it really doesn't have to be this way.

In this chapter, we have drawn on our years of research into territory, personal space and the importance of seating arrangements and our extensive knowledge of building relationships and dealing with conflict to help you plan a Christmas that is as merry and peaceful as possible. Concentrate on the here and now, follow our advice and this Christmas will be memorable for all the right reasons.

'One of the nice things about Christmas is that you can make people forget the past with a present.'
ANON.

Festive Cheer

No matter where you are spending Christmas or with whom, we all have something in common – everyone wants to enjoy the festive season (even that nit-picking aunt who seems determined to find fault with everything you do). The best way to ensure that Christmas is pleasurable and fun is to show your guests and relatives that you are having a good time yourself. And how do you do that? Simple: by smiling.

Smiling tells another person you are non-threatening and asks them to accept you on a personal level. Lack of smiling explains why many dominant individuals, such as James Cagney, Clint Eastwood, Margaret Thatcher and Charles Bronson, always seem to look grumpy or aggressive and are rarely seen smiling – they simply don't want to appear in any way submissive.

*Contrary to popular belief, 'festive cheer' isn't
the sound you make as you watch your relatives
drive away on Boxing Day.*

Furthermore, smiling at someone has been found to make people smile back at you, which causes positive feelings in both you and them. Professor Ruth Campbell, from University College London, believes there is a 'mirror neuron' in the brain that triggers the part responsible for the recognition of faces and expressions and causes an instant mirroring reaction. In other words, whether we realise it or not, we automatically copy the facial expressions we see. Even a fake smile has this effect – something we'll look at in more detail in Chapter 9. One thing is certain: if you want people to feel relaxed and to smile more at Christmas, the best thing *you* can do is to smile.

Why the Jokes in Christmas Crackers Are Good for You

*What do you call Santa's little helpers?
Subordinate clauses.*

*What do you get if you eat Christmas decorations?
Tinsilitis.*

*Why are chocolate buttons rude?
Because they are naked Smarties.*

*What is Santa's favourite pizza?
One that's deep pan, crisp and even.*

We're all familiar with Christmas-cracker jokes. They usually range from terrible to just bad, but even so, reading them out, groaning and laughing (even if you're laughing at how atrocious they are) can have a very positive effect on you and your relationships with those around you.

As we touched on in Chapter 5, when laughter is incorporated as a permanent part of who you are, it builds relationships, improves health and extends life. When we laugh, every organ in the body is affected in a positive way. Our breathing quickens, which exercises the diaphragm, neck, stomach, face and shoulders. Laughter increases the amount of oxygen in the blood, which not only helps healing and improves circulation, it also expands the blood vessels close to the skin's surface. This is why people go red in the face when they laugh. It can also lower the heart rate, stimulate the appetite and burn up calories – something that can come in very handy when we are overindulging on Christmas Day.

Neurologist Henri Rubenstein found that one minute of solid laughter provides up to 45 minutes of subsequent relaxation. Professor William Fry at Stanford University reported that 100 laughs will give your body an aerobic workout equal to that of a ten-minute session on a rowing machine. Medically speaking, this is why a damn good laugh at Christmas is damn good for you.

The older we become, the more serious we become about life. An adult laughs an average of 15 times a day; a pre-schooler laughs an average of 400 times.

Laugh Your Way to a Happy Christmas

Even if Christmas is not going exactly as you'd planned or hoped, or if family circumstances or even a bereavement have filled Christmas with negative associations, there is evidence that smiling can make you feel happier. Research shows that people who laugh or smile, even when they don't feel especially happy, make part of the 'happy zone' in the brain's left hemisphere surge with electrical activity. In one of his numerous studies on laughter, Richard Davidson, professor of psychology and psychiatry at the University of Wisconsin in Madison, hooked subjects up to EEG (electroencephalograph) machines, which measure brainwave activity, and showed them funny movies. Smiling made their happy zones click wildly. He proved that intentionally producing smiles and laughter moves brain activity towards spontaneous happiness.

....
The secret of a happy Christmas is in being happy.
....

Arnie Cann, professor of psychology at the University of North Carolina, discovered that humour has a positive impact in counteracting stress. Cann led an experiment with people who were showing early signs of depression. Two groups watched videos over a three-week period. The group that watched comedy videos showed more improvement in their symptoms than did a control group that watched non-humorous videos.

Try to smile and laugh as much as possible with your family over Christmas – watch a comedy together, read out the jokes in Christmas crackers and play charades and funny board games. It will have an extremely positive effect on building relationships with your family, will make others and yourself feel generally happier, fight stress and, because it burns calories, will even help prevent you from developing a stomach like Father Christmas's!

Why You Feel Claustrophobic at Christmas

When you invite people to spend the festive period with you, you throw open your doors, welcome your relatives in . . . and then wonder how you could have forgotten how much hard work it is having guests staying in your home. Your house can start to feel uncomfortably small and full, and other people's clutter can begin to grate on you. Your guests may be perfectly charming and helpful, but you may still find yourself feeling claustrophobic and easily irritated. Why is this?

'Claustrophobia' is the feeling you get at Christmas when your relatives tell you they've decided to stay until New Year. 'Claus-trophobia' is the fear of Santa Claus.

One of the problems at Christmas is that you are suddenly thrown together with family members who you are perhaps not accustomed to spending extended periods of time with. The problem is not simply that you are different; it is that the other person or people are invading your personal space and territory, just as you are theirs. At Christmas, when you spend long periods of time with relatives, it results in a sense of claustrophobia, feeling irritated when somebody helps themselves to something in your home or even feeling trapped when a relative stands too close to you.

'At Christmas, my home is your home . . . up to a point.'

Even if you are visiting relatives in their own home, you may still feel that they are invading your personal space. Our Intimate Zone (15–45 centimetres) is normally entered by a close relative or friend. People who don't know you so well will stand further away. Over a period of days, having a relative standing so close may start to feel unwelcome. This is perfectly natural. Try to take breaks – perhaps go for a walk or pop out on your own. This will help to prevent tension from building up.

'You're Sitting in My Chair'

A territory is an area or space around a person that he claims as his own, as if it were an extension of his body. In the cinema, it's an armrest where we do silent battle with strangers who try to claim it. A person's home, office and car also represent a territory, each having clearly marked boundaries in the form of walls, gates, fences and doors. Each territory may have several sub-territories. For example, in a home a person's private territory may be their kitchen and they'll object to anyone invading it when they're using it; and Dad has his shed in the garden. These areas are usually marked either by leaving personal possessions on or around the area, or by frequent use of it. A family member might mark his or her favourite chair by leaving a personal object, such as a handbag or magazine, on or near it to show their claim and ownership of the space.

At Christmas, when we invite people into our home, these unspoken boundaries are frequently crossed – the mother-in-law who takes over the cooking, the uncle who sits in 'your chair', the brother who flicks channels with the remote control.

....

'Santa Claus has the right idea.
Visit people only once a year.'
VICTOR BORGE

....

Try the Luncheon Test
To see how important these boundaries are, try this simple test next time you eat with someone. Unspoken territorial

rules state that a table is divided equally down the middle and the host will carefully place the salt, pepper, sugar, flowers and other accessories equally on the centre line. As the meal progresses, subtly move the salt cellar across to the other person's side, then the pepper, flowers and so on. Before long this subtle territorial invasion will cause a reaction in your lunchmate. They either sit back to regain their space or start pushing everything back to the centre. Be warned, though: don't try this test on Christmas Day!

'Where Would You Like Me to Sit?'

When a person claims a space or an area among strangers, such as a place at the conference table or a towel hook at the health club, he does it in a predictable way. He usually looks for the widest space available between two others and claims the area in the centre. In the same way, when we are around those with whom we are familiar – for example, relatives at Christmas – we tend to choose our seats in a predictable way. At Christmas dinner, it would probably be considered rude and presumptuous for a guest to sit uninvited at the head of the table. In fact, we are so aware of the importance and etiquette of where we sit that often guests will ask the hosts where they would like them to sit.

Where people sit at Christmas dinner says a lot about the individual relationships and power struggles between you.

The male of the house – the husband or father – will more often than not sit at the head of the table at Christmas dinner. The partner who is taking charge of the cooking will generally sit nearest the kitchen. This is not simply so that he or she can nip to the kitchen easily – it also indicates the kitchen to be their domain. This person is sending out a message to show that they are in charge of that area. If a son has invited his parents to Christmas dinner, it is not uncommon for him to offer his father the seat at the head of the table and to ask him to carve as a way of demonstrating that he is still deferential to him.

A simple question such as, 'Which chair is yours?' can avoid the negative results of a territorial error.

Dealing With Difficult Guests

Even with the best will in the world, and the best intentions, sometimes our relatives seem determined to create tensions or leave all the hard work to us.

....

Peace on Earth: spare a thought for the 26 per cent of people in an ICM poll who responded that 'There is bound to be some kind of argument in my household at Christmas.'

....

Most of us have a relative who we find challenging. It might be a meddling sister-in-law, the uncle who insists on getting drunk and causing arguments or the niece and nephew who refuse to behave. But whoever that particular person is, there are strategies you can employ that will make the festive get-together more harmonious and pleasurable.

The Guest Who Takes Over Your Home

As we learned above, territory can be a contentious issue at Christmas. Most of us will be familiar with the guest who takes over our home in some way. This is the guest who scatters their possessions and opened Christmas presents across your house and seems to have little respect for your personal space. He or she bulldozes their way through Christmas and your home. This can leave you feeling taken for granted or even threatened.

Sometimes people do this intentionally. If somebody took a place at the head of the table at Christmas dinner without asking, it could well be seen as a way of asserting dominance. Similarly, the mother-in-law who sits herself in the daughter-in-law's seat is essentially saying, 'I am the woman of the house.'

Leaning against something or touching something can also be used as a method of dominance or intimidation if the object belongs to someone else. If a guest in your home on Christmas Day were to sit in your favourite armchair as soon as you welcome him in, put his feet up on your coffee table and pick up one of your magazines, you would consider this quite presumptuous, if not intimidating.

An easy way to intimidate someone is to sit on or use their possessions without their permission. At Christmas, for instance, a relative might change the CD on your CD-player, or a teenager might sit on the kitchen worktop while talking to you. If you know the guest very well and feel comfortable, this could simply be an indication that he is relaxed in your home, but if the person is less familiar to you and the gesture seems inappropriate, he could be consciously trying to send a message to you. Be aware that the way somebody treats your home at Christmas can reveal a lot about their attitude towards you.

We stake a physical claim
on what we believe is ours.

The Guest Who Won't Help Out

People often complain that some guests don't help enough at Christmas. They expect you to entertain them, run around after them and don't seem to notice your pleas for help. You might ask them to peel some vegetables and they don't register. You might request they do the washing-up but they are too busy having a good time to listen.

Our expectations of what Christmas should be are set as a child and some adult guests seem to revert to childhood over the festive period – expecting the host or hostess to do everything possible to ensure that Christmas is a special day for them, with little or no regard for how Christmas is for you. This is often true of siblings or grown-up children, who think they can return to an idyllic childhood and let you take care of everything. While you may be happy to do this up to a point, every guest should pull their weight to some degree.

If you want to be listened to but don't want to cause tension, there is a very simple but effective body-language technique that can be used here. Palm Power is one of the least noticed, but most powerful, body signals to use when giving someone directions or commands. When employed in a certain way, Palm Power invests its user with the power of silent authority.

There are three main palm command gestures: the Palm-Up position, the Palm-Down position and the Palm-Closed-Finger-Pointed position. Given that it is Christmas and you want to persuade the guest to help without antagonising them, it is important that you use the appropriate gesture.

The differences between the three positions are shown in this example: it's Christmas Day and your grown-up younger brother is treating your house like a hotel. He has eaten your food, drunk your wine and not lifted a finger to help. You and your partner have cooked and catered for the whole family, are worn out and want him to help with the washing-up. We'll assume that you use the same tone of voice, the same words and facial expressions in each example, and that you change only the position of your palm.

The palm facing up is used as a submissive, non-threatening gesture, reminiscent of the pleading gesture of a street beggar and, from an evolutionary perspective, shows the person holds no weapons. Your brother will not feel he is being pressured into washing up and is unlikely to feel threatened by your request. The Palm-Up gesture became modified over the centuries and gestures like the Single-Palm-Raised-in-the-Air, the Palm-Over-the-Heart and many other variations developed.

When the palm is turned to face downwards, you will project immediate authority. Your brother will sense that you've given him an order to wash up. This may, however, have the effect of making him feel that he is being ordered about.

The Nazi salute had the palm facing directly down and was the symbol of power and tyranny during the Third Reich. If Adolf Hitler had used his salute in the Palm-Up position, no one would have taken him seriously – they would have laughed.

Now imagine that you had asked your brother to wash up but at the same time used the Palm-Closed-Finger-Pointed, which is a fist where the pointed finger is used like a symbolic club with which the speaker figuratively beats his listeners into submission. Subconsciously, it evokes negative feelings in others because it precedes a right over-arm blow, a primal move most primates use in a physical attack. If you had done this, your brother would undoubtedly have had a very negative reaction to you.

The Palm-Closed-Finger-Pointed gesture is one of the most annoying gestures anyone can use while speaking, particularly when it beats time to the speaker's words. In some countries such as Malaysia and the Philippines, finger pointing at a person is an insult, as this gesture is only used to point at animals. Malaysians will use their thumb to point to people or to give directions.

If you want your brother to respond receptively to your request, be sure to use the Palm-Up position. To demonstrate how effective it can be, we conducted an experiment with eight lecturers who were asked to use each of these three hand gestures during a series of ten-minute talks to a range of audiences and we later recorded the attitudes of the participants to each lecturer. We found that the lecturers who mostly used the Palm-Up position received 84 per cent positive testimonials from their participants, which dropped to 52 per cent when they delivered exactly the same presentation to another audience using mainly the Palm-Down position. The Finger-Pointed position recorded only 28 per cent positive response and some participants had walked out during the lecture.

When asking a reluctant guest to help out this Christmas, try using the Palm-Up position – it will bestow you with silent authority.

The Palm-Up position can also be used to good effect when trying to get overexcited or unruly children to calm down at Christmas. In short, if you want somebody to do something at Christmas, use the Palm-Up position – it shows that you are being respectful but are making a request and appealing for their help.

The Critical or Disruptive Guest

We probably all have a relative who seems determined to make life difficult for us at Christmas. They may be the critical or superior type who finds fault with everything you do – for example, last Christmas your aunt complained there was no bread sauce so you made it specially this year, only for her not to eat any because she says she wants to lose weight. She then helps herself to trifle *and* Christmas pudding. Or the difficult guest may be the type to get drunk, become outspoken and even cause an argument, ruining the day for everyone.

One way to deal with guests who like to ruin Christmas dinner is to use a height advantage to help establish the fact that they are *guests* in your home. Historically, raising or lowering the height of your body in front of another person has been used as a means of establishing superior-subordinate relationships. We refer to a member of royalty as 'Your Highness', whereas individuals who commit unsavoury acts are called 'low', 'low down' and 'low-lifes'. The protest-rally speaker stands on a soapbox to be higher than everyone else, the judge sits higher than the rest of the court, the Olympic gold-medal winner stands higher than the other medal winners, those who live in a penthouse command more authority than those who live at ground level, some cultures divide their social classes into the 'upper class' and 'lower class', and pharmacists stand 45 centimetres above everyone else. And everyone understands the significance of standing to speak to a meeting to gain control.

Try the Floor Test

If you want to test the authority that goes with height, try this exercise with a friend. First, lie on the floor and get your friend to stand over you to maximise the height difference. Next, ask your friend to reprimand you as loudly and forcefully as he can. Then change positions – you stand, he lies down – and ask him to repeat his reprimand. You'll find that not only does he find it nearly impossible to do, his voice will sound different and he'll lack any authority while trying.

How to Use Height to Your Advantage at Christmas

We all know that children are generally sat on lower seats at the table – in spite of the fact that they are smaller already.

Seating children on lower seats (and sometimes on a lower table) separates them from the adults. In the case of disruptive or critical guests, you can employ a similar strategy to neutralise their power over you. When you arrange the dining area ready for Christmas dinner, set up a space where you can control the environment by having chairs of varying heights and ask the 'problem people' to sit on the lower chairs. Sitting neutralises height and sitting the Incredible Hulk on a low sofa diminishes his perceived power. You will probably notice that the disruptive or critical people become less vocal.

If you have a guest who you know is prone to ruining Christmas for others, try seating them on a lower chair and watch how they become more submissive.

Sitting at opposite ends of a table also evens things up, as does standing and leaning against something – staking your claim on your territory – while they are seated.

How Body Lowering Can Sometimes Raise Status

There are some circumstances in which lowering your body can be a dominance signal. This happens when you slouch down and make yourself comfortable in an easy chair in another person's home while the owner is standing. It's the complete informality on the other person's territory that communicates the dominant or aggressive attitude.

If you are going to someone else's house for Christmas, note that a person will always be superior and protective on his own territory, especially in his own home, and so practising submissive gestures and behaviour is effective for getting the person on side with you.

The Argumentative Guest

This guest loves to have debates at Christmas and will argue about everything and anything. They may not see their behaviour as argumentative – and may refer to it as 'healthy debate' – but if you're not careful, Christmas can descend into a family feud. Rather than worrying about how to control and calm down your unruly guest, look at how your seating plan can have an impact on their behaviour.

Where you sit in relation to other people is a powerful way of obtaining cooperation from them. We conducted surveys with seminar delegates during the 1970s, 1980s and 1990s to determine which positions at a table they felt gave the best result for communicating specific attitudes. We did this by delegate involvement at seminars and by using survey questionnaires from our database. The first major study in seating positions was conducted by psychologist Robert Sommer from the University of California, who analysed a cross-section of students and children in public and social situations such as bars and restaurants. We applied Sommer's findings to seating positions at a dining table. While there are marginal differences between cultures and the relationships between people, we have summarised here the seating positions you will encounter most of the time. In the following examples, we have assumed that you are using a rectangular table, which is the most common shape for a dining table.

The Corner Position

In this position, you sit the argumentative guest on one side of a corner of the table and you – or another person who is good at pacifying or calming – on the other side of the corner. This position is used by people who are engaged in friendly, casual conversation. It allows for good eye contact and the opportunity to use numerous gestures and to observe the gestures of the other person. The corner of the table provides a partial barrier in case one person begins to feel threatened, and this position avoids territorial division of the table. In this position, you can relieve a tense atmosphere and increase the chances of a positive outcome.

The Competitive/Defensive Position

Let's say you have two argumentative or disruptive guests and sit them opposite each other at Christmas dinner. In this seating arrangement, competitors face each other, just like Western gunslingers. Sitting across the table from a person can create a defensive, competitive atmosphere and can lead to each party taking a firm stand on his point of view because the table becomes a solid barrier between both parties. If you choose this seating plan, you had better expect fireworks. In a work environment, this position is taken by people who are either competing with each other or if one is reprimanding the other. It can also be used to establish a superior-subordinate role. We found that, in business scenarios, people speak in shorter sentences from the Competitive/Defensive position, can recall less of what was said and are more likely to argue.

Avoid sitting argumentative guests directly opposite each other on Christmas Day.

If you sit yourself or another person whose aim is to pacify directly opposite the argumentative guest, with the aim of diffusing an argument, the Competitive/Defensive position reduces the chance of a successful negotiation. More cooperation will be gained from the Corner position than will ever be achieved from the Competitive/Defensive position. Conversations are significantly shorter and more pointed in the Competitive/Defensive position. It is clearly a bad choice for Christmas Day.

Perfecting Your Christmas Seating Plan

As we have seen in the above example of the argumentative guest, seating positions should not be accidental: placing certain people in specific positions can affect how successful Christmas Day is. A good seating plan can not only help avoid arguments but develop relationships and encourage shy guests to open up. When you devise a seating plan, ask yourself, who is the person you want to control or influence most (you may want to build a relationship with your mother-in-law, or ensure that your younger brother doesn't shock your grandmother with his risqué jokes), and where is the best position to sit to achieve this? Who is most and least likely to want to argue or oppose? If there is no appointed leader – for example, if you are having Christmas dinner at a restaurant with your sister and brother-in-law, rather than in your home – who has claimed a seating position to give themselves the most power? The answers to these questions will help ensure Christmas Day runs smoothly and will prevent controlling or difficult guests from taking over.

Firstly, consider the shape of your table. Below we will detail the common shapes of table and assess the impact they will have on how merry your Christmas is.

Rectangular Tables

On a rectangular table, it seems to be a cross-cultural norm that the person seated at the head of the table has always commanded the most influence. When there is a rectangular table at Christmas dinner or another formal meal, it is traditional for the 'man of the house' to be seated at the head. Strodtbeck and Hook set up some experimental jury deliberations that revealed that the person sitting at the head position was chosen significantly more often as the leader. When two people are seated at opposite ends of the table – for instance, in the case of the man and the father or father-in-law – the most influential person tends to sit at the end opposite the door – let's call this person A, and opposite him, with their back to the door, person B, is perceived as being next in the hierarchy. Interestingly, the person (or persons) seated directly next to person A – we'll call him person C – is perceived as being third in the hierarchy, as they are directly next to person A. Positions A and B are perceived as being task-oriented – they will undertake roles such as carving and serving the turkey. In some households, Position B will be taken by a woman – she is seen as having a strong role, but because her husband is in Position A, she is still less influential than him. Position D is seated on the side of the table, next to person C. This is seen as being occupied by an emotional leader, often a woman, who is concerned about group relationships and getting people to participate.

A rectangular table is probably the most common shape for a dining table – partly because it uses least space – but it is not necessarily the best option. Think carefully about who sits where. For a trouble-free Christmas, do not sit argumentative people directly opposite each other. Rectangular tables create a competitive or defensive relationship between people because each person has equal space, equal frontage and separate edges. It lets everyone take a 'position' on a given subject and allows more direct eye contact.

Square Tables

Some families choose a square table for dining. These are ideal for having short, to-the-point conversations, and can be useful in some business contexts, but are not so good for a harmonious Christmas.

....

Square tables belong in a canteen,
not in your home on Christmas Day.

....

If you have to use a square table, bear in mind that most cooperation comes from the person seated beside you, and the one on the right tends to be more cooperative than the one on the left.

Historically, the person on the right is less likely to be able to successfully stab you with their left hand, hence the 'right-hand man' is more favoured and others subconsciously credit the right-hand person with having more power than the one on the left side. Most resistance comes from the person seated directly opposite in the 'gunslinger' position, and when four people are seated, everyone has someone sitting opposite.

Let's assume that you have invited your wife's parents for Christmas Day. You have a square table and don't know where best to seat everyone. You get on well with your father-in-law but have a problematic relationship with your mother-in-law. In order to develop your relations with her, the best position to seat her would be on your right-hand-side because this is the best place to develop cooperation. As you get on well with your father-in-law, it is acceptable for you to sit opposite him without any chance of dispute.

Circular Tables

If possible, a round table is definitely the best option for Christmas dinner. King Arthur used the Round Table as an attempt to give each of his knights an equal amount of authority and status. A round table creates an atmosphere of relaxed informality and is ideal for promoting conversation among people who are of equal status, as each person can claim the same amount of table territory.

A round dining table is the ideal shape for a friendly, relaxed Christmas.

The circle itself has become a worldwide symbol of unity and strength, and simply sitting in a circle promotes the same effect. Unfortunately, King Arthur was unaware that if the status of one person is higher than the others in the group, it completely alters the dynamics of group power. The king held the most power and this meant that the knights seated on either side of him were silently granted the next highest amount of power, the one on his right having more than the one on his left. The power then diminished relative to the distance that each knight was seated away from the king.

The knight seated directly opposite King Arthur was, in effect, in the Competitive/Defensive position and was likely to be the one to give the most trouble. Sixty-eight per cent of respondents saw the person sitting directly opposite them on a round table as the one most likely to argue or be competitive. If you often argue with your father, and you are sitting in the King Arthur position, do not position him opposite you on Christmas Day. When sitting directly beside another person, 71 per cent said they were either having a friendly conversation or cooperating.

The round table, often a coffee table with wraparound seating or lower chairs, is used to create an informal, relaxed atmosphere or to persuade. It is also often found in families that practise democracy or don't have a dominant parent, but can be exercised to good effect in any family at Christmas.

....

The shape of a family dining-room table can give a clue to the power distribution in that family, assuming that the dining-room could have accommodated a table of any shape and that the table shape was selected after considerable thought. 'Open' families go for round tables, 'closed' families select square tables and 'authoritative' types select rectangular tables.

....

The Quiet or New Guest

If one of your Christmas guests is prone to be quiet or introverted, or if you are introducing someone new – perhaps a neighbour, or your son's new girlfriend, whom you know to be shy – try placing that person at the head of the table, furthest from the door with their back to a wall. If it is a rectangular table, we recommend that you sit at the other head of the table – so that they don't feel that they are being presumptuous. You could also sit them immediately on the right of the person at the head of the table – i.e. you or your partner if you are hosting Christmas. You will be amazed to see how simply placing a person in a powerful seating position encourages them to begin to talk more often and with more authority and how others will also pay more attention to them.

Christmas tip: to encourage a shy guest to open up, sit them on the right of the person at the head of the table.

An Experiment in Learning

In a classroom, pupils who are most eager to learn and participate tend to sit closest to the front and those who are least enthusiastic sit in the back or to the sides. If you are spending Christmas Day with someone who is very shy and does not become involved in conversation easily, try sitting them near the people who tend to participate most and observe the effect this has on them. Some presenters and trainers have abandoned the 'classroom-style' meeting concept for training smaller groups and replaced it with the 'horseshoe' or 'open-square' arrangement because evidence suggests that this produces more participation and better recall as a result of the increased eye contact between all attendees and the speaker. The same can be observed at the Christmas dinner table.

Three's Company

When there are just three people at Christmas dinner, it is not uncommon for one party to feel excluded. They may be naturally quiet or feeling slightly uncomfortable. Perhaps you and your partner have invited an elderly relative or one parent, or perhaps you are spending Christmas Day with your parents who are separated. If this is the case and you are seated at a circular table, there is a simple strategy you can employ to make sure that the third party feels equally involved in conversation. Let's assume that you, person C, are going to talk with persons A and B, and that you are sitting in a triangular position at the table. Assume that person A is talkative and asks many questions and that person B remains silent throughout. When A asks you a question, how can you answer him and carry on a conversation without making B feel excluded? Use this simple but effective inclusion technique: when A asks a question, look at him as you begin to answer, then turn your head towards B, then back to A, then to B again until you make your final statement, looking finally at A again as you finish your sentence. This technique ensures B feels involved in the conversation at Christmas.

How to Make Your Guests Feel Relaxed

Every host wants their guests to feel at home and relaxed at Christmas. If you're worried that people might be a little on edge – unsurprisingly, bringing two families or divorced parents together can make everyone a little uncomfortable – and you want to make sure they feel at ease, it might help to understand a little about our evolution.

A hundred thousand years ago, ancestral man would return with his kill at the end of a hunting day and he and his group would share it inside a communal cave. A fire was lit at the entrance to the cave to ward off predators and to provide warmth. Each caveman sat with his back against the wall of the cave to avoid the possibility of being attacked from behind while he was engrossed in eating his meal. The only sounds that were heard were the gnashing and gnawing of teeth and the crackle of the fire. This ancient process of food sharing around an open fire at dusk was the beginning of a social event that modern man re-enacts at barbecues, cook-outs and dinner parties. Modern man also reacts and behaves at these events in much the same way as he did over a hundred thousand years ago.

Now that we understand a little of our history, let's look at how this can be applied to the modern Christmas Day meal. If you have a particularly tense or nervous guest, have him sit with his back to a solid wall or screen. Research shows that respiration, heart rate, brainwave frequencies and blood pressure rapidly increase when a person sits with his back to an open space, and we breathe more quickly as our body readies itself for a possible rear attack, particularly where others are moving about – at Christmas, when we are juggling cooking turkey and all those countless trimmings, there is bound to be lots of activity. On no account should you sit your nervous guest with his back towards an open door or a window at ground level, as this will further increase tension. Only do this if you want to unnerve or rattle someone!

....

Christmas tip: sit a nervous guest with their back to the wall rather than to an open space – it will help him to relax.

....

Next, the lights should be dimmed and muffled background music – perhaps some classical Christmas melodies – should be played to relax the senses. Many top restaurants have an open fireplace or fire facsimile near the entrance of the restaurant to recreate the effects of the fire that burned at the ancient cave feasts. Light some candles on the Christmas table – perhaps an advent candle – for a similar effect and your guest will immediately feel more relaxed and at ease.

Avoiding Arguments at Christmas

Between three and six o'clock on Christmas Day is statistic-ally the time when most family get-togethers are inclined to become heated. According to new research from Somerfield, one in three Brits settle down for some festive fireworks at 4.17 p.m. – overeating, tiredness and drinking too much doubt-less play a large part in this.

Despite being 'social' animals, we are bound to have areas where we will disagree and irritate each other. The secret is to remain calm and to accept that people won't always get along. The best cure for arguments at Christmas is prevention – keep an eye on how much you and others drink, avoid top-ics of conversation that you know to be triggers for feuds, follow our advice about seating plans and keep people occu-pied with helping out (peeling vegetables, passing round drinks, etc.) and playing games, as busy people are less likely to argue than when they are just sitting around. The annual argument over the remote control – Grandma wants the Queen's Speech, your son wants to watch *The Snowman*, your sister wants *Coronation Street*, your uncle's rooting for the latest Bond film and you don't care because nobody can hear the TV over your father's snoring – can be resolved by sharing. Decide early on in the day what you'd like to watch, and record anything that clashes.

....

In a poll in 2004 by ICM/Guardian, more than one in four people said they expected there to be some kind of argument in their home over Christmas.

....

Coping With Children

Christmas is all about children – it is for them and because of them. You want to spoil children at Christmas and make sure they have a wonderful time. But if you don't want an over-excited, overtired child, souped up on sweets, you also need to make sure that they abide by some basic principles. If you have other people's children in your home, be clear about what is acceptable and what isn't. And the very best thing you can do to make sure children stay content at Christmas? Don't forget to buy plenty of batteries!

....

'I once bought my kids a set of batteries for Christmas with a note on it saying, "Toys not included."'
BERNARD MANNING

....

Chapter 7

THE OTHER WOMAN
AT CHRISTMAS

For many people, one of the hardest aspects of Christmas is not the endless shopping, cooking, cleaning, writing cards and wrapping presents, it's the fact that their mother-in-law comes to stay. As we saw in Chapter 6, other family members – grandmothers, aunts and brothers – also come high on the list of unwelcome guests, but, on this the most special day of the year, the mother-in-law, or the monster-in-law, is in a league of her own. Her arrival is so dreaded, her visits such agony that we decided she needed a chapter all to herself.

'Every Christmas I get an awful pain that stays for a week. Then my mother-in-law goes back to her own home.'

Mothers-in-law probably inspire more jokes than any other group of people on earth. They are constantly the butt of humour by comedians, between men and in TV sitcoms, consistently characterised as witches, battleaxes or shrews. Remember, it was one of the founders of Soviet Russia, Lenin, who, when asked what should be the maximum penalty for bigamy, replied, 'Two mothers-in-law.'

My mother-in-law called by this morning. When I answered the door she asked, 'Can I stay here for a few days?'
'You certainly can,' I replied – and closed the door.

One year, a particularly harried husband decided to buy his mother-in-law a cemetery plot as a Christmas gift.
The next year, he didn't buy her a gift. When she asked him why, he replied, 'Well, you still haven't used the gift I bought you last year!'

But while mothers-in-law do indeed prove a problem in many people's marriages, with up to a third who break up blaming the mother-in-law for the rift, it's not usually the woman's mother who causes most of the problems. Our research finds, time and time again, that it's the man's mother who is the real danger. His mother-in-law may provoke the most public complaints, but these are usually more tongue-in-cheek than protesting about some real problem.

I received an email today advising that my mother-in-law had passed away and asking whether to arrange a burial, a cremation or embalming.
I replied, 'Be sure – arrange all three.'

Difficult mothers-in-law aren't a major problem for most men. Even for the legendary Giovanni Vigliotti of Arizona, who enjoyed 104 marriages between 1949 and 1981 in his own name and 50 aliases, those 104 mothers-in-law were far less of a problem than the 34 years in jail he received as a result.

'I can always tell when the mother-in-law's coming to stay; the mice throw themselves on the traps.'
LES DAWSON

A man's mother-in-law might irritate him, nag him and exasperate him, but most men don't usually dislike them. Mother-in-law problems don't dominate men's lives and they don't ruin many Christmases.

There's an old Polish proverb 'The way to a mother-in-law's heart is through her daughter.' Most men realise this. What most women's mothers want, more than anything, is to see their daughters happy. And if the men in their lives make them happy, they're unlikely to cause problems.

If they're going to have problems with their in-laws at Christmas, it's far more likely to come from their father-in-law refusing to let go of his cherished 'princess'. There simply aren't many father-in-law jokes – they're just not a laughing matter.

His Mother – Her Problem

The real dramas in most families come from the man's mother, the female partner's mother-in-law. Research carried out by Utah State University showed that in over 50 per cent of all marriages there were real problems between the daughter-in-law and her husband's trouble-making and recalcitrant mother.

'Every year there's only one thing standing between me and a happy Christmas – my husband's mother.'

While not all mothers-in-law deserve this fearsome reputation, to many daughters-in-law a meddling, possessive and intrusive mother-in-law who won't cut the umbilical cord with her son can be soul-destroying. It can quite literally ruin Christmas. And for some women, mother-in-law crises often seem unmanageable and unsolvable, and can cause misery, anguish and, ultimately, the threat of divorce.

A man met a wonderful woman and became engaged. He arranged to have dinner with his mother that evening so she could meet his new fiancée. When he arrived at her home, he took three women – a blonde, a brunette and a redhead. His mother asked why he had brought three instead of just one. He said he wanted to see if his mother could guess which woman was her future daughter-in-law. She looked at each one carefully and then replied, 'It's the redhead.'

'How did you work it out so quickly?' he asked.

'Because,' she replied, 'I can't stand her.'

Many mothers ruin their sons for the next women in their lives. They mother them, cook, clean, wash and iron for them. They believe they are showing their sons love with these acts, but they are actually causing problems for their sons in later life when they develop relationships with women. The sons, in the end, find it hard to do the things their mothers did for them.

It's a tough one for the female partner in a relationship to deal with, but instead of criticising his mother, it's actually far more effective to train him to do what she wants him to do, and stop blaming his mother. He is now an adult and must be responsible for his own actions.

These problems can be very complex, for we have a three-way relationship, which can vary from being one in which all three people seem to be emotionally well balanced, independent, unselfish and caring, to one where one, two or all three individuals may be motivated by jealousy, possessiveness, dependence, immaturity, selfishness or emotional instability.

'When my mother-in-law comes to visit at Christmas, I lose the will to live.'

Even if a woman has managed to develop a strong three-way relationship with her partner and her mother-in-law, old problems can often resurface at Christmas when the mother-in-law comes to stay. She is essentially entering the daughter-in-law's territory and there may be a power struggle as a result. If a woman can get on with her mother-in-law over Christmas, she can survive anything.

....

Eighteen per cent of Brits – men and women – dread their partner's mother spending Christmas in their home.

....

They're Not All Bad

Not all mothers-in-law live up to the dreaded reputation of wickedness. While the Utah State University research shows that approximately 50 per cent of mothers-in-law are seen as troublemakers, the other 50 per cent must be either neutral at worst or loving, helpful and generous members of the extended family. And, often, mothers-in-law are blamed for the shortcomings and emotional problems of their sons or daughters-in-law.

It's important to bear in mind that mothers-in-law are in a difficult position because the daughters-in-law usually have a close bond with their own mothers and will regularly discuss with them, in detail, every little thing. It's normal that a girl will rely more on her own mother than on her mother-in-law. This can cause jealousy on the part of her partner's mother. This can be particularly problematic at Christmas, when a daughter might invite her own mother as well as her mother-in-law. Seeing how well a daughter gets on with her own mother can make a mother-in-law feel particularly vulnerable and like an outsider.

Mothers-in-law are always thinking about what their sons

are doing, especially if he is their only child and their life is boring. Is he eating properly? Is the house clean enough for him? etc., etc. But sons rarely talk with their mothers about anything. Consequently, a mother-in-law will rarely get much information and begins to feel excluded from her son's new family and may think the only way she can be included is to force her way in. This means that at Christmastime, when a mother-in-law is staying in her son's home, she may try to assert her presence by offering advice, however unwelcome, taking over chores and dominating in the kitchen, all of which can be seen by the daughter-in-law as 'sticking her nose in'. During courtship, a man's girlfriend will often work hard at building a relationship with his mother because it is a good strategy to keep her onside. When marriage makes things more permanent, however, it almost becomes like two women fighting over one man.

But for every problem there is a solution. What is needed is the willingness to solve it. The son and daughter-in-law must tackle the situation openly and maturely if they want to have a peaceful Christmas and a good relationship.

First Christmas in Your Own Home

Spending your first Christmas in your own home is an important milestone for any couple. It signifies that you are adults and are comfortable with each other and in your own surroundings. Unfortunately, it is often a particularly hard step for a couple with a demanding mother-in-law. There comes a time when any son must break away and decide to no longer spend Christmas at 'home'. For some mothers, this is a difficult time, as it means that he is no longer their little boy. As a consequence, many clingy mothers-in-law will try to reassert control once in their son and daughter-in-law's home – perhaps by sitting in the daughter-in-law's usual seat at Christmas dinner, criticising decorations, the cooking or the cleanliness of the home or simply helping out too much to the point where the daughter-in-law sees it as a criticism. This is a challenging time for everyone and the couple are going to have to learn to set some boundaries.

Our lives are becoming busier and busier and there is less and less time for our immediate family, let alone our extended family; less time for human contact. It can be very difficult for our generation to handle our parents and both sides need to be understanding and come up with solutions if everyone is going to be happy. The parents need quality time and the children need time for their immediate family. Where, in the past, extended families all lived in the same house, now we may live in another village, another town or even another country. Making the effort is part of family life. This is what Christmas is all about, and if you know the rules, you really can learn to have the happy, harmonious Christmas you desire.

> *'I like to have plenty of notice of when my mother-in-law is going to arrive at Christmas, so that I have enough time to book a holiday for then.'*

The 'Helpful' Mother-in-Law

Sometimes a mother-in-law is intrusive because she is *too* helpful at Christmas – serving other people at Christmas dinner, offering the cranberry sauce round too enthusiastically, running after her son and tidying up after him and suggesting the children get off to bed early on Christmas Eve are all classic examples. This may be motivated by the best intentions, but it can have a detrimental effect on the whole family. In one study, researchers found that a common source of conflict is the battle over who is 'mum' in the family. At Christmas, the key issues are who has final say over all those things most women still dictate: what you're going to eat, what time Christmas dinner will be and children's table manners. This can have two effects. Firstly, it can make the daughter-in-law feel guilty and that she is somehow inadequate as a wife and mother. Secondly, if a mother-in-law 'mothers' her son over Christmas and spoils the children, it can make it more difficult for a wife to get her husband to help out around the home and her children back into their usual routine when her mother-in-law returns to her own home.

Case Study: Susan, John and Cassie

Susan's Perspective

Susan was in her early forties when her husband left her. 'Good riddance!' she told her friends. He drank too much and never really cared about his family. But she still had her son, John. He was an honest young man of 22, and he would look after her.

Susan thought that John wasn't interested in girls. She had provided him with every care, comfort and emotional support, what could he possibly see in another woman? She felt John realised that just as she had raised, cared and loved him since his birth, it was now his responsibility to look after her. At Christmas, though, she got particularly lonely and so she wanted to be around her son and spend as much time as possible with him.

Cassie's Perspective

Cassie liked John as soon as she met him. While they were courting, however, she felt it strange that he didn't take her home to meet his mother until after they had announced their engagement. Susan wasn't particularly welcoming, but Cassie just thought she needed time to adjust.

It wasn't until after their marriage, however, that Cassie realised she had inherited the mother-in-law from hell. The problems started immediately after Cassie and John returned from their honeymoon. Susan would call in most days, completely unannounced.

Cassie and John really wanted to spend their first Christmas as a married couple in their new home. John didn't want Susan to be on her own for Christmas – he'd never spent Christmas without her – and so Cassie agreed to invite Susan to stay for a few days. Susan wanted to stay for longer and persuaded John to allow her to stay for two weeks.

Cassie tried to be friendly and welcoming, but she soon tired of being told by Susan what John liked to eat for Christmas dinner, how to cook the turkey and repeatedly being told how hard John worked. Susan found fault with almost everything that Cassie did and didn't thank her or compliment her on any of her hard work with decorating the house and cooking.

Over the course of the festive season, their relationship deteriorated. Susan found fault with the present that Cassie had bought her, gave Cassie chocolates for Christmas when she knew she was on a diet, repeatedly criticised her cooking and would take over in the kitchen. No matter what Cassie did around the house, Susan always had a 'better' way of doing things. In several instances Susan commented on how dirty the house was and took it upon herself to clean it. She also smoked inside even though she knew Cassie would prefer she didn't. Cassie felt pushed out of her first Christmas in her own home and interpreted Susan's interference as a personal slight. It was as though Susan was trying to make her feel like a bad wife. The atmosphere became extremely tense.

Even though it was Christmas, Cassie started to avoid spending time with her mother-in-law, making excuses to do chores and to leave the house, but Susan would use this as an opportunity to talk endlessly with her son. She would reminisce with John about their 'best ever' Christmas. She would ask when he was coming 'home' to paint the house or take her shopping. Her requests seemed endless. Susan even arranged with John that next year they would spend Christmas at her home and have a 'proper family Christmas'. Susan had effectively replaced her husband with her son. Cassie felt increasingly excluded. She had given up Christmas with her own parents to spend it with John's mother. She felt like she would never be good enough no matter how hard she tried, and she started to feel that John was married to his mother, not her. The mother-in-law from hell had turned Christmas into the Christmas from hell.

Cassie tried to discuss the problems with John, but he felt that Cassie was simply being possessive and that his mother was only trying to help by helping in the kitchen and offering alternative ways of doing things. He also felt that it was his responsibility to look after his mother's needs. Eventually, Cassie tired of the arguments and fumed in silence, but she refused to allow Susan to stay in their home for Christmas again.

....

One survey revealed that an astonishing 40 per cent of British people have such bad experiences with family staying over for Christmas that they vow never to invite them again.

....

John's Perspective

John felt he had a great relationship with his mother. She never criticised him; in fact she felt that everything he did was absolutely wonderful. The only problem John had was that whenever he brought a girlfriend home, their relationship soon cooled off after meeting his mother. But when he met Cassie, he knew he was in love. He decided to keep Cassie away from his mother as much as possible.

After John and Cassie married, Susan was always around, helping out. Over Christmas Susan was a great help and her advice was invaluable – there is so much to organise for Christmas that it can get stressful, so he was glad that his mother was there to lend a hand. But Cassie seemed completely unwilling to take advice, and was always arguing with Susan and complaining endlessly to John about his mother. He loved Cassie but she was driving him nuts with her emotional outbursts. Having a typical problem-solving male brain, John thought that this was his Christmas holiday and he shouldn't have to spend it solving arguments between his wife and his mother. He began to think that life would be less complicated if he was single again.

✳

This drama is not uncommon and unfortunately tensions all too often come to a head at Christmas, when mother-in-law and daughter-in-law encroach on each other's personal space. The season of goodwill can turn into a battleground. Mothers-in-law in particular can feel very competitive, as they see their traditional role – as mother, host, cook – being usurped by someone younger. Consequently, they react by trying to reassert their authority. This is essentially a struggle for status.

Christmas can become a power struggle between mother-in-law and daughter-in-law as each tries to gain status in the home.

It is played out in families the world over. In some countries, the problems are worse than others. In Russia, where young married couples live with parents because apartments are rarely available, a strong culture of mother-in-law hatred has arisen. In Spain, there is a disease known as *suegritis*, an illness said to be caused by mothers-in-law.

Both parties must forge a bond if their lives are to work, and they are to be able to enjoy the festive season. Women did this naturally for survival in the cave and need to do it now for survival in the modern world, for a stress-free life and to avoid dragging men into the problems. Women need to sort this relationship out between themselves without getting their husbands or sons involved. Men may actually enjoy the attention of having two women fighting over them and while this continues it feeds their egos. The wife needs to be clever enough to take control of the situation and ensure that problems are dealt with strictly between her and her mother-in-law. When this works it is a win-win situation. The last thing a woman needs is her mother-in-law complaining about her to her husband; she really needs an ally rather than an enemy.

......

'I told my mother-in-law that my house was her house, and she said, "Get the hell off my property."'

JOAN RIVERS

......

How to Resolve Problems With Your Mother-in-Law This Christmas

Naturally, these sorts of problems are best sorted out long before Christmas, so that both parties have time to put changes in place before problems have a chance to come to a head. That way, by the time Christmas comes round, both mother-in-law and daughter-in-law will have found a way to coexist happily.

If problems are cropping up early on in a relationship, then the daughter-in-law, by necessity, has to be the one to try and build bridges. She has to realise that time is limited between the courtship and marriage, and, while all her attentions have been focused on her primary relationship, it's likely that if she invests no time at all in the relationship with her potential mother-in-law, there will be a negative dividend. She should try and spend some time with her alone, so the mother-in-law sees her as an individual in her own right, rather than as simply the spouse. Strengthening that relationship on a one-on-one basis will lead to fewer problems when there are more people involved.

Later on in a marriage, if problems have been allowed to take root, however, it's actually very difficult to settle on a workable agreement between three people, each of whom have different agendas and priorities. One side will rarely yield to what they perceive as an alliance between the other two. At this stage, therefore, the problem must be solved by the two most affected parties – the son and the daughter-in-law.

The first questions that they need to answer are:

❉ Do they both recognise that a problem exists?
❉ Do they want a happy, loving and long life together?
❉ Do they want to solve the problem?

If the answer is 'No' to any one of these questions, marriage-guidance counselling is recommended. If the answer is 'Yes', the husband and wife should sit down and commit to paper exactly what they feel the problems are.

In the case study above of the Christmas from hell, for example, Cassie could write:

❉ Susan outstays her welcome at Christmas. I invited her for a few days and she came for two weeks.
❉ Susan is always critical and has no confidence in my abilities. She takes over at Christmas and is domineering.
❉ Susan demands too much attention from John, so he does not spend enough time with me.
❉ Susan smokes inside and doesn't respect the fact that she is just a guest in John's and my home.

John, on the other hand, could write:

❉ My mother is lonely at Christmas, but Cassie doesn't care.

✳ My mother tries to help Cassie and has more experience in doing things at Christmas, but Cassie refuses to accept valuable advice.
✳ I don't understand why everyone is frustrated all the time, when all I want to do is get along with everyone and enjoy Christmas.

The problem, then, is Cassie's and John's. Susan does not have the problem. She has been allowed to maintain her control of John and through him she controls Cassie. Ultimately she controls everyone's Christmas. John has never severed the umbilical cord between him and his mother. He hasn't really left 'home' yet and has not matured.

....

The best time to cut an umbilical cord is at birth.

....

Cassie is also an unwitting participant here. She has helped become the architect of her own misery. She did not set limits on Susan when she saw problems first emerging. She has, in effect, let Susan rampage boundlessly through her marriage and home. It is little wonder that Christmas has become a territorial dispute.

Setting Boundaries at Christmas

Setting boundaries means deciding ground rules and drawing lines others are asked not to cross. Boundaries were not laid down by John and Cassie when they first married. This is a very easy trap for young people to fall into. They are inexperienced and have usually lived within other people's boundaries. They are not assertive and usually feel that other family members are only trying to help with their advice. This meant that when they had their first Christmas at home, Susan was able to take over.

Setting boundaries and being assertive are two vital lessons that young married people must learn. When boundaries have been set, everyone knows how far they can go. They know that if they step outside the boundaries, they will invite trouble. Within their marriage, Cassie and John would have boundaries, lines that cannot be crossed even with each other, so why not have boundaries for Susan too? Boundaries must be laid down for Christmas just as they can be laid down for the rest of the year.

Cassie claims that Susan takes over in the kitchen at Christmas, so Susan needs training in crossing this boundary. She must be told that she values her help but it would be appreciated if she would not take over. With regard to the housework, Susan has again crossed an unset boundary. Cassie must be assertive. She needs to thank Susan for her efforts but state that she and John are happy to take care of the housework themselves. She also needs to explain that it is her and John's home, not her's, and as much as she is welcome here, they do not wish her to smoke inside. Understandably, Susan will feel rebuffed and hurt, but that's her problem. It must be pointed out that they don't love her any less but these are the boundaries. Susan will eventually get over it and adjust.

The problem of Susan wanting John to work around her home is also a boundary problem. John does have a responsibility to help her but an agenda needs to be agreed by Cassie. The three of them should talk it through at a time when emotions aren't running high – preferably before or after Christmas. It might even be a solution to talk to a handyman in the area, and give Susan the phone number. John and Cassie could even offer to pay his bill for a year as a combined birthday and Christmas present. Cassie could offer to participate to help Susan feel part of the family.

*'I enjoyed Christmas for the first 30 years of my life.
Then my mother-in-law appeared on the scene.'*

John also needs to take responsibility for how long his mother stays at Christmas. She may want to stay for two weeks but this is going to place a lot of pressure on all of them. John should invite his mother for a week at most – less if he can. If she asks to stay for longer, he should explain that it is important to him that he and Cassie spend more time together at Christmas and that they have their own lives to get on with. He can also help his mother develop her own interests outside his family. This could include such activities as lawn bowls, a reading group, becoming a hospital volunteer, joining a retirees' club, taking a course, or helping at an organisation like Meals-on-Wheels. Both John and Cassie should be ready to take a real interest in her 'new' life until it assumes a momentum of its own.

*'I always encourage my mother-in-law to go for a
nice refreshing walk on Christmas Day. My hope is
that one year she'll keep on walking.'*

Every single one of Cassie's problems can be solved by setting out boundaries and insisting they be observed. It's not easy. Susan will be upset initially, and may even lash back with guilt claims and emotional blackmail such as 'You don't care that I'm lonely at Christmas.' Such tactics, however, will only work if you let them. You know you're right to be doing what you're doing, you've talked it through thoroughly, you've examined all the possible responses and you're ready to deal with them. People can only succeed in making you feel guilty if you agree to accept that guilt.

Cassie must remember that this is her Christmas just as

much as anyone else's. She needs to take responsibility for making herself happy. As we have seen, if she holds resentment inside without taking positive action, it will only surface in other ways and the outcome is a miserable Christmas for everyone.

Mother-in-law: an anagram of Woman Hitler.

If Cassie and John tackle their boundary-setting exercise with Susan using empathy and love, a sound adult and enjoyable relationship will ultimately, inevitably, grow. And, at the end of the day, if all these efforts do not solve the problem and Susan continues to ruin Christmas, they may just have to not invite her for Christmas any more. She has to understand that she has to meet them halfway.

Chapter 8

MISTLETOE AND STOCKINGS: SEDUCTION, DATING AND SEX

....

'Let's be naughty and save Santa the trip.'
GARY ALLAN

....

Christmas is the best time of year for single people to explore the dating potential around them. Most of us have office parties, family gatherings and other functions to attend over Christmas, making the festive period an optimum time for meeting new people and approaching those who have already caught our eye. Research shows that more couples go on first dates at the beginning of January – having met over Christmas and New Year – than at any other time of year. Subscriptions to online dating rise dramatically during December, and dating companies report that events are often oversubscribed because so many singles are keen to have fun and meet new people over the festive period. In one poll, nearly three-quarters of London-based single respondents claimed that finding love is at the top of their Christmas wish list, and it also tops the New Year's resolutions for singles.

....

According to a survey carried out for Trebor Mints, the British will exchange 'around 600 million kisses a day over Christmas – that's 25 million an hour, 417,000 a minute and 6,940 every second'.

....

Despite the fact that love may be in the air for singles and new couples, however, established couples are less likely to be in the mood for romance and sex at Christmas than at any other time of year.

In this chapter, we'll look in detail at the subject of seduction and sex at Christmastime. We have used our research into attraction and seduction and our own experience to show you how you can attract and be attractive to someone you meet at a Christmas party or event, and how you can ensure that you find someone with whom you'll want to spend not just this Christmas, but *every* Christmas. And we'll also look at why married couples and those in long-term relationships shun sex over the festive period and what you can do to put the sparkle back into Christmas.

Why Women Have Got Seduction All Wrapped Up

When it comes to seduction – whether it's at Christmas or at any time – women really have got it all wrapped up. Dr Simon Baron-Cohen at Cambridge University conducted some tests where subjects were shown photographs in which only a narrow strip of the face across both eyes was visible. The subjects were asked to choose between mental states expressed in the photographs such as 'friendly', 'relaxed', 'hostile' and 'worried' and attitudes such as 'desire for you' and 'desire for someone else'.

Statistically, pure guesswork would result in half the answers being correct, but men's average score was 19 out of 25, while women scored 22 out of 25. This test shows that both sexes have a greater ability to decode eye signals than body signals and that women are better at it than men.

The success women have in intimate encounters is directly related to their ability to send courtship signals to men and to decode those being sent back. For a man, success in the mating game relies mainly on his ability to read the signals being sent to him, as opposed to being able to initiate his own moves. Most women are aware of courtship signals, but men are far less perceptive, often being completely blind to them, which is why so many men have difficulty finding potential mates. Women's difficulty in finding partners is not about reading signals, it's more about finding a man who'll match their criteria.

Ask any man who usually makes the first move in courtship and he will invariably say that men do. All studies into courtship, however, show that women are the initiators 90 per cent of the time. A woman does this by sending a series of subtle eye, body and facial signals to the targeted man, who, assuming he is perceptive enough to pick them up, responds to them.

At Christmas, when it comes to seduction, it's women who have the twinkle in their eye.

There are men who will approach women in a club or bar without being sent the green light, but while some of these men are regularly successful with finding partners, their over-all statistical success rate is low because they weren't invited first – they're simply playing the numbers game.

Worst Christmas chat-up line: 'Can I get a picture of you so I can show Santa exactly what I want for Christmas?'

If you're a single man at a Christmas party, your best approach is to study women's eye signals and body language if you want to find that someone special.

How to Grab a Man's Attention at a Christmas Party

You're at a friend's Christmas party and have spotted the man you secretly fancy on the other side of the room. The question is, how do you get his attention? The secret is in the eyes. Most women try to grab a man's attention by meeting his gaze, holding it for two to three seconds, then looking away and down. This gaze is long enough for her to send him a message of interest and potential submission.

> *Christmas tip: to grab a man's attention at a Christmas party, meet and hold his gaze.*

However, an experiment by Monika Moore, PhD, of Websters University, showed that most men are not hardwired to read a woman's first gaze signal so she usually needs to repeat it three times before the average man picks up on it, four times for really slow men and five or more times for the especially thick. When she finally gets his attention, she will often use a small version of the Eyebrow Flash – that is a small, subtle eye-widening gesture that tells him the signal was intended for him. The eyebrows rise rapidly for a split second and then drop again. This is an unconscious signal that acknowledges the other person's presence and which translates to 'I acknowledge you and am not threatening.'

If a man doesn't seem to notice, sometimes a simple face-to-face verbal approach of 'Hey, I like you!' is more effective on men who are slow on the uptake.

How Men's Fires Get Lit

Lowering the eyelids while simultaneously raising the eyebrows, looking up and slightly parting the lips is a cluster that has been used by women for centuries to show sexual submissiveness. This is one of the trademarks of the sex sirens such as Marilyn Monroe, Deborah Harry and Sharon Stone, and is another good seduction tip to use this Christmas.

Not only does this gesture maximise the distance between the eyelid and eyebrows, it also gives the person a mysterious, secretive look, and new research shows that this is the expression many women have on their faces immediately before having an orgasm.

Mistletoe magic: according to one survey, Christmas is 'top of the kissing calendar': 73 per cent of us will kiss under the mistletoe, and only 15 per cent will kiss on Valentine's Day.

Does Alcohol Make Everyone Look More Attractive at Christmas?

As well as mistletoe, increased alcohol intake may partly explain why single people are more likely to approach the opposite sex at Christmas, but this only seems to apply to men. In a study carried out in singles bars, researchers found that the later the hour, the more attractive the available women looked to the unattached men. A woman who was rated by the men as a five out of ten at 7 p.m. was rated seven by 10.30 p.m. and eight and a half at midnight, with alcohol levels enhancing the scores. With women, however, a man who rated a five at 7 p.m. was still given the same mark at midnight.

For a woman, a man who rates a five at 7 p.m. still rates the same score at midnight, regardless of how much she's had to drink.

Alcohol did not increase his attractiveness rating, and, in some cases, it even decreased his rating. So be warned: if you're wearing reindeer antlers and a novelty Christmas tie, a woman is not going to be attracted to you, no matter how much she's had to drink.

Women still evaluate a man's viability as a partner by his personal characteristics above his physical appearance, regardless of the hour or the amount of alcohol consumed. Men increase a woman's attractiveness rating relative to the odds that she will let him carry out his role as a professional sperm donor.

First Date at Christmas – Some Surefire Tips for Men

Given that there are so many couples going on first dates at Christmas, we thought we had better share some festive dating advice. Women don't have a problem when it comes to love and romance, but most men are in the dark about it so they simply make sure they're ready for love any time, any place. A man's romantic skills (or lack thereof) play a significant part in whether a woman will feel like having sex with him, so here are six tried and tested things that work as well for men today as they did 5,000 years ago.

1 Set the environment. When you consider a woman's sensitivity to her surroundings and the high receptivity of her senses to outside stimuli, it makes sense that a man pays attention to the environment. Women's oestrogen hormones make her sensitive to the right lighting – dimly lit rooms make pupils dilate, so people look attractive to each other and skin blemishes and wrinkles are less noticeable. A woman's superior hearing means the right music is important, and a clean, secure cave is better than one that can be invaded by children or other people at any moment. Women's insistence on sex in

private explains why most women's private fantasy is of having sex in public, while a man's private fantasy is sex with a stranger.

2 Feed her. Having evolved as a lunch-chaser, you'd think it would occur to a man that providing a woman with food stirs up primal female feelings. This is why taking a woman to dinner is a significant event for her even when she's not hungry because the provision of food shows his attention to her well-being and survival. Cooking a meal for a woman has an even deeper intrinsic meaning as it brings out primitive feelings in both a man and a woman.

3 Light a fire. Collecting wood and lighting a fire to give warmth and protection has been done by men for women for hundreds of thousands of years, and appeals to most women's romantic side. Even if it's a gas fire that she can light easily herself, he needs to light it if he wants to set a romantic atmosphere. The pay-off comes from the act of providing for her needs, not from the fire itself.

4 Bring flowers. Most men do not understand the power of a bunch of fresh flowers. Men think, 'Why spend so much money on something that will be dead and thrown out in a few days?' It makes sense to a man's logical mind to give a woman a pot plant because, with constant care and attention, it will survive – in fact, you could even make a profit on it! However, a woman doesn't see it that way – she wants a fresh bunch of flowers. After a few days the flowers die and are thrown out, but this presents an opportunity for him to buy another bunch and once again bring out her romantic side by providing for her needs.

5 Go dancing. It's not that men don't want to dance, it's just that many of them don't have the location in the right brain required to feel rhythm. Go to any aerobics class and watch the male participants (if any turn up) trying to keep time. When a man takes dancing lessons for basic rock 'n' roll and waltz, he will be the hit of the

party with all women. Dancing has been described as a vertical act of horizontal desire and that's its history – it's a ritual that evolved to allow close male-female body contact as a lead-up to courtship, just as it did with other animals.

6 Buy chocolates and champagne. This combination has long been associated with romance, although few people know why. Champagne contains a chemical not found in other alcoholic beverages that increases testosterone levels. Chocolate contains phenylethylamine, which stimulates a woman's love centre in the brain. Recent research by Danielle Piomella at the Neurosciences Institute in San Diego discovered three new chemicals called N-acylethanolamines, which attach themselves to the cannabis receptors in a woman's brain, giving her sensations similar to being high on marijuana. These chemicals are in brown chocolate and cocoa, but not in white chocolate or coffee.

Finding a Partner for Life, Not Just for Christmas

It's Christmas Eve and you've met that someone special. Love starts with lust, which can last a few hours, a few days or a few weeks. By Valentine's Day you've moved to the next stage of love – infatuation – which lasts, on average, 3–12 months, but by the end of the summer attachment, the final stage, has taken over. By the following Christmas the blinding cocktail of hormones has subsided, and a year after meeting you see each other in the cold light of day and those little habits you found so endearing at first begin to become irritating. Last year, you thought those reindeer antlers he wore were cute; now you want to rip them off and tell him to grow up. Last year, he loved hearing you talk about your Christmas plans (what you're doing, what you're buying people, what your

New Year's resolutions are . . .); now he's contemplating murder. You silently ask yourself, 'Can I live like this for the rest of my life? What do we have in common?'

The flower of love is the rose. After three days all the petals fall off and you're left with an ugly, prickly thing.

Chances are you don't have much in common or much to talk about. Nature's objective is to throw men and women together under the influence of a powerful hormonal cocktail that causes them to procreate and not think. Finding the right partner means deciding what things you will have in common with someone in the long term – someone you want to be with this Christmas, next Christmas and every Christmas after that – and to do this in advance of nature's blinding hormonal highs. When infatuation has passed – and pass it will – can you maintain a lasting relationship based on friendship and common interests? Write a list of the traits and interests you want in a long-term partner and then you'll know exactly who you are looking for.

A man will have a list of qualities for his ideal mate, but when he goes to a party, especially a Christmas party, when he is feeling particularly outgoing and on a natural high, his brain is fired up by testosterone. It then searches for the 'ideal' woman based on hormonal motivation – nice legs, flat stomach, round bum, good breasts and so on, all features connected with short-term procreation. Women want a man who is sensitive and caring, has a V-shaped torso and a great personality, all things connected to child-rearing, lunch-chasing and protecting. These are also short-term biological needs and have little to do with success in a modern relationship. When you write a list of the desirable long-term characteristics in your perfect partner and keep it handy, it helps you to be objective about a new person the next time nature tries to control your thoughts and urges.

It's relatively easy to find someone you want to spend time with this Christmas, but the secret is to find someone you want to spend *every* Christmas with. Nature wants you to procreate as often as possible and it uses powerful drugs to push you into it. When you understand this and are armed with a job description of your ideal long-term mate, you are less likely to be tricked and more likely to be successful in your hunt for that elusive perfect partner with whom you'll be finally able to live happily ever after.

Christmas Parties – How to Go as a Couple (and Return as One)

Once you've found that special person, the work doesn't stop there . . .

Barbara and Allan were getting ready to go to a Christmas cocktail party. Barbara had bought a new dress and was anxious to look her best. She held up two pairs of shoes, one blue, one gold. Then she asked Allan the question that all men fear: 'Darling, which should I wear with this dress?'

A cold chill ran down Allan's back. He knew he was in trouble. 'Ahh . . . umm . . . whichever you like, sweetheart,' he stammered.

'Come on, Allan,' she said impatiently. 'Which looks better . . . blue or gold?'

'Gold!' he replied nervously.

'So what's wrong with the blue?' she asked. 'You've never liked them! I paid a fortune for them and you hate them, don't you?'

Allan's shoulders slumped. 'If you don't want my opinion, Barbara, don't ask!' he said.

He thought he'd been asked to fix a problem, but, when he solved it, she wasn't at all grateful. Barbara, however, was using that typical female speech trait, indirect speech. She'd already decided which shoes she was going to wear and didn't want another opinion on it; she wanted confirmation that she looked good.

If you're a man in a couple and are going to a Christmas party, take our advice: if a woman asks, 'Blue or gold?' when selecting shoes, it's important that a man does not give an answer. Instead, he should ask, 'Have you chosen a pair, darling?' Most women are taken aback by this approach because most men they know immediately state a preference.

'Well . . . I thought I could possibly wear the gold . . .' she'll say uncertainly. The reality is, she has already chosen the gold shoes.

'Why the gold?' he'll ask.

'Because I'm wearing gold accessories and my dress has a gold pattern in it,' she'll respond.

A skilled man would then reply, 'Wow! Great choice! You'll look fabulous! You've done well! I love it!'

You can bet that you will have a great time at the Christmas party.

Christmas Parties – How to Give a Woman a Sincere Compliment

It's Christmas Eve and a husband and wife are getting ready to go out to a Christmas party. The wife is standing in front of a full-length mirror taking a hard look at herself.

'You know, dear,' she says, 'I look in the mirror and I see an old woman. My face is all wrinkled, my hair is grey, my shoulders are hunched over, I've got fat legs, and my arms are all flabby.' She turns to her husband and says, 'Tell me something positive to make me feel better about myself.'

He studies hard for a moment, thinking about it. He desperately wants to give her a compliment, so he says in a soft, thoughtful voice, 'Well, there's nothing wrong with your eyesight.'

So that's how not to do it! If you're going to a Christmas party and want to make the woman in your life feel special, it's important that a man learns how to give a sincere compliment. When a woman tries on a new dress and asks a man, 'How does it look?' she'll probably receive a simple response like 'Good' or 'Fine', which does not score any points. To score good points, a man needs to respond the same way a woman would: by giving details. Some men cringe at the thought of responding in detail, but if you are prepared to try it, you will score big points with most women.

For example, if he said, 'Wow! Great choice! Turn round, let me see the back. That colour really suits you! The cut flatters your figure. Those earrings match your outfit perfectly. You look wonderful,' most women would be extremely impressed, and it will make her Christmas.

> *To make a woman feel special at Christmas, don't just tell her she looks good — tell her why she looks good.*

Couples and Sex at Christmas

The presents are unwrapped, you're pleasantly full with mince pies and turkey, the children are asleep upstairs, and Christmas is nearly over for another year. For the first time in ages you have the opportunity to unwind and spend some time with each other, and yet surveys reveal that the very last thing on couples' minds on Christmas Day is making love. Why is this? What effect does stress have on your sex drive? Is it the same for men as it is for women? And why do men buy lingerie as Christmas presents?

> *In one survey, 70 per cent of men said that they had less sex in December than in any other month.*

Before we answer these questions, we need to understand a little about the science behind sex. Your sex centre is located in the hypothalamus, which is the part of the brain that also controls the emotions, heart rate and blood pressure. It's about the size of a cherry, weighs around 4.5 grams and is larger in men than in women, homosexuals and transsexuals.

This is the area in which hormones, particularly testosterone, stimulate the desire for sex. Considering that men have 10–20 times more testosterone than women and a larger hypothalamus, it's obvious why the male sex drive is so powerful. This is the reason men can have sex virtually any time and in almost any place – whether it's three o'clock in the morning on Christmas Day or not. Add to this the social encouragement that men have received for generations to 'sow their oats' and society's disapproval of sexually active women, and it's little wonder the differences in attitude to sex have always been a bone of contention between men and women (no pun intended).

Sex and Christmas Stress

We are often asked what the effect of planning for Christmas and all that stress has on a couple's sex drive. Firstly, it must be said that men and women have different sex drives, and most couples experience different levels of sex drive at different times in their week, month and year. It may be fashionable to suggest that modern men and women are equally interested in sex, or that normal couples are perfectly matched sexually, but that's not the way it is in real life.

Overall, most men have a higher sex drive than most women. A study at the Kinsey Institute, world leaders in human sex research, showed that 37 per cent of men think about sex every 30 minutes. Only 11 per cent of women think of it as often. For a man, a continual high dose of testosterone keeps his drive high and this is why, when it comes to sex, he's ever ready.

....

Studies carried out on American university campuses showed that when an attractive woman approaches a man and asks him to go to bed with her, 75 per cent say 'Yes', whereas no women said 'Yes' when approached by an attractive man.

....

Testosterone is the main hormone that creates the feeling we call sex drive and love is a combination of chemical and electrical reactions. Those who think that love is all in the mind are partially correct. For women, the psychological factors such as trust, closeness and overall well-being all combine to create the conditions under which the hormone cocktail is released by the brain. Men can release this cocktail any time, any place.

....

When it comes to sex, women need a reason; men need a place.

....

Many people might think that we are more likely to have sex at Christmas – all that mistletoe must surely have an effect. But according to one recent poll, the festive season makes us less inclined to have sex, not more. We all know that Christmas can be a stressful time. Unfortunately, because a woman's sex drive is affected by psychological factors, her desire to have sex is significantly affected by events in her life. If she has had a long, hard day at work, it's late on Christmas Eve, she has 17 people coming to Christmas dinner, the kids are sick, and she's still struggling to put together a My Little Pony Castle as a present to her daughter from Santa, sex will not even be a consideration. All she can think about is getting to Boxing Day in once piece, and when she finally drags herself to bed, it will be to sleep.

'The one thing women don't want to find in their stockings on Christmas morning is their husband.'
JOAN RIVERS

When the same events happen to a man, he sees sex as a sleeping pill – a way of releasing the built-up tensions of the day. He may be equally stressed out by Christmas preparations, but he wants an outlet for his tensions, so at the end of the day, he puts the hard word on the woman, she calls him an insensitive moron, he calls her frigid and he spends Christmas Eve sleeping on the couch. Sound familiar?

Interestingly, when men are asked about the state of their relationship, they usually discuss it in terms of their partner's personal services on the day they were asked – for example, at Christmas, whether she cooked him breakfast or gave him a nice present. Women describe the condition of the relationship based on recent events – for example, how attentive he's been over the last few months, his helpfulness around the house and how much he has communicated with her. Most men don't understand this difference. He may have been a perfect gentleman all day, done all the Christmas chores, bought her a fantastic present, but she refuses sex because she's still unhappy that he insulted her mother two weeks ago.

One remarkable study found that the level of criticism and contempt displayed by a couple towards each other bears a direct relation to the number of infectious diseases from which they would suffer over the next five years, especially in the women. The higher the level of criticism, the more prevalent and virulent the infections. The reason for this is that heightened stress levels resulting from arguments weakens the immune system, making the body more susceptible to disease and less able to cope.

What Else Affects How Much We Make Love at Christmas?

A recent poll carried out by Ann Summers revealed that nearly six out of ten men and women said that they were less likely to have sex at this time of year because they had consumed too much food or drink.

The three stages of man:
He believes in Santa Claus.
He doesn't believe in Santa Claus.
He is Santa Claus.

As well as stress, rows and fatigue play a role. Seven out of ten men said the amount of sex they had in December dropped to an annual low, and 90 per cent of women said their sexual appetite plunged throughout the holidays due to worrying about Christmas shopping.

Even having relatives to stay and staying at relatives' houses can inhibit couples' sex drives – 66 per cent of couples said that they avoided having sex at Christmas for fear of being overheard. Despite the tradition of kissing under the mistletoe, it seems that sex and romance don't feature highly on couples' agenda at Christmas.

In a poll carried out by Ann Summers, 72 per cent of respondents said they had argued with their partner about their in-laws at least once over Christmas. What's more, 63 per cent felt this argument had put them off making love.

Why Men Buy Sexy Lingerie for Women as Christmas Presents

We may have less sex at Christmas, but men are still clearly thinking about it – many women ask us why their husbands buy them sexy or erotic lingerie for Christmas. To answer this question, we need to explain to you what is called the 'Rooster Effect'.

A rooster is a very randy male bird that can copulate with hens almost incessantly – more than 60 times in a given mating. He cannot, however, mate with the same hen more than five times in one day. By the sixth time he completely loses interest and can't 'get it up', but if he is presented with a new hen, he can mount her with the same enthusiasm he did with the first – this is the 'Rooster Effect'.

A bull will lose interest after copulating seven times with the same cow but can be fired up again by the introduction of a new one. By the time he reaches the tenth new cow, he is still giving an impressive performance. A ram will not mount the same ewe more than five times but can continue to mount new ewes with tremendous zeal. Even when the ram's former sexual partners are disguised with perfume or bags over their heads, the ram still cannot perform. You just can't fool them. This is nature's way of ensuring that the male's seed is spread as widely as possible in order to achieve the highest number of conceptions and ensure the survival of that species.

Men give their penis a name because they don't want a stranger making 99 per cent of their decisions for them.

For healthy young men, the number is also around five. On a good day, he can have sex with the same woman five times but will usually fail to give a sixth encore. Introduce a new female, however, and, like roosters and bulls, his interest (along with parts of his anatomy) can rapidly rise.

A man's brain needs variety. Like most male mammals, a man is pre-wired to seek out and mate with as many healthy females as possible. This is why men love novelty factors like sexy lingerie in a monogamous relationship. Unlike other mammals, men can fool themselves into believing they have a harem of different women by dressing their partners in a range of sexy clothing and lingerie. It is, in effect, his version of putting a bag over her head to provide a variety of different appearances. Most women know the effect lingerie has on men, although few understand why it is so powerful.

Every Christmas the lingerie sections of department stores are full of men sheepishly skulking around trying to find a sexy gift for their partners. In January, those women are standing in line at the refunds counter in the same store. 'This is just not me,' they say, 'he wants me to dress up like a hooker!' The hooker is, however, a professional sex seller who has researched market demands and is packaged to make a sale. One American study has shown that women who wear a variety of erotic lingerie have generally much more faithful men than women who prefer white cotton underwear. This is just one way that a man's urge for variety is sometimes addressed in a monogamous relationship.

According to a survey in 2002 by MSN Shopping, one in six women has been bought 'sexy' underwear for Christmas by their partner that leaves them cold because they consider it too tacky or tarty.

All He Wants for Christmas – Why Men Can't Help Themselves

Men's enthusiastic and impulsive sex drive has a clear purpose – to ensure that the human species continues. Like most male mammals, he had to evolve with several elements for its success. Firstly, his sex drive had to be intensely focused and not easily distracted. This would allow him to have sex under almost any conditions, such as in the presence of potential threatening enemies, or in any place where a sexual opportunity presented itself.

A man needed to be able to ejaculate as often as possible in the shortest space of time to avoid being caught by predators or enemies.

He also needed to spread his seed as far afield and as often as possible. The Kinsey Institute in the US reported that without society's social rules, they believe nearly all men would be promiscuous, as 80 per cent of all human societies have been for most of human existence. Since the arrival of the age of monogamy, however, men's biological urge has caused constant mayhem for couples trying to build a relationship and is the number-one cause of modern relationship problems.

Male sex urge is so strong that Dr Patrick Carnes of the Sexual Recovery Institute in Los Angeles estimates that up to 8 per cent of men are addicted to sex, compared with less than 3 per cent of women.

All She Wants for Christmas – Why Women Are Faithful

As we learned earlier, a woman's hypothalamus is much smaller than a man's, and she only has small amounts of testosterone to activate it. This is why women, overall, have significantly lower sex drives than men and are less aggressive. So why didn't nature create woman as a raving nymphomaniac to ensure continuation of the species? The answer is in the long period of time it takes to conceive and to raise a child to self-sufficiency.

....

A woman wants lots of sex with the man
she loves. A man wants lots of sex.

....

There's a small percentage of women who are as promiscuous as men, but their motivation is usually different to that of men. To be turned on sexually, the brain circuitry of the nest-defending human female responds to a range of criteria other than just the promise of sex. Most women want a relationship or at least the possibility of some emotional connection before they feel the desire for sex. Most men don't realise that once a woman feels an emotional bond has been created, she will happily bonk his brains out for the next three to six months. With the exception of the rare percentage of nymphomaniacs, most women feel the strongest urge for physical sex during ovulation, which can last several days or several hours.

Male sex drive is like a microwave – it ignites instantly and operates at full capacity within seconds, and can be turned off just as quickly when the meal is cooked. Women's sex drive is like an electric oven – it heats slowly to its top temperature and takes a lot longer to cool down.

Beware the Office Christmas Party

Where does marriage fit into the lifestyle of an animal species that has a biologically promiscuous male?

Promiscuity is wired into a man's brain and is a legacy of his evolutionary past. Throughout human history, wars greatly diminished the numbers of men, so it made sense to add to the size of the tribe as often as possible. The number of men returning from battle was usually lower than at the start. This meant that there was always a large number of widows, so creating a harem for the returning males was an effective survival strategy for the tribe.

Giving birth to boys was seen as a wonderful event because additional males were always needed to defend the community. Girls were a disappointment because the tribe invariably had an excess of females. This is the way it was for hundreds of thousands of years. In addition, modern man is still equipped with a large hypothalamus and enormous amounts of testosterone to fulfil his ancient urge to procreate. The reality is that men, like most primates and other mammals, are not biologically inclined to complete monogamy.

It has to be understood, however, that in discussing men's urge to be promiscuous, we are talking about biological inclinations. We are not promoting promiscuous behaviour or providing men with an excuse for infidelity. We live today in a world that is completely different to that of our past, and our own biology is often completely at odds with our expectations and demands.

Human biology is dangerously out of date.

Unfortunately, Christmas can put temptation in the way of married men. It is a sad fact that if a man is going to cheat on his wife, it is likely to be with a work colleague. Studies reveal that along with the Internet, the workplace ties as being the number-one place for instigating extramarital affairs. And, emboldened by alcohol and carried away by the excitement of the festive season, there is evidence to suggest that the office Christmas party is the place where men are most likely to make their move on female colleagues who have caught their eye over the previous year.

In an independent survey of 1,000 male UK office workers, two-thirds of respondents claimed to have kissed a colleague at the office Christmas party.

Men's Health magazine carried out a survey of 1,000 male office workers and found that 44 per cent of respondents had had an affair with a co-worker at one time in their life at the office Christmas party. In the same survey, carried out in 1999, 40 per cent of young men (under-35s) said they were looking for 'action' at that year's Christmas party, and 57 per cent of all married men admitted to having an affair with a work colleague. These are worrying statistics.

Three recent surveys have revealed that Christmas office parties are breeding grounds for workplace affairs.

One solution to preventing a workplace affair at the office Christmas party, or stopping one in its tracks, would be for wives to turn up to the party with their husbands. But men must take responsibility for their own actions. The fact that something may be instinctive or natural doesn't mean that it's good for us. The brain circuitry of a moth gives it an instinctive attraction towards bright lights and this allows the moth to navigate at night using the stars and the moon. Unfortunately, the modern moth is also living in a world that is dramatically different to the one in which it evolved. We now have moth- and mosquito-zappers. By doing what is natural and instinctive, the modern moth flies into the zapper and is incinerated instantly. In understanding their biological urges, modern men have a choice of avoiding self-incineration as a result of doing what comes naturally.

Why Do Men Ogle Other Women at Christmas Parties?

Robert and Sue were very happily married and had just arrived at a Christmas Eve party. As they were getting some drinks, Robert happened to notice an attractive woman in a 'Mrs Santa Claus suit' and glanced her way. Sue turned immediately to Robert, looked him full in the face and, without appearing to move her lips, said, 'If you don't stop staring at her, I'm leaving.' Robert couldn't believe that Sue had seen him looking at the other woman when he believed he had looked at her so briefly and so discreetly – it was like Sue had eyes in the back of her head. Sue couldn't believe that he could make it so obvious that he was looking at another woman.

Women often catch men out when they are looking at other women because they have wider peripheral vision than men. As we learned in Chapter 5, as a nest-defender, a woman has brain software that allows her to receive an arc of at least 45 degrees clear vision to each side of her head and above and below her nose, while, as a hunter, men's larger eyes are configured for long-distance tunnel vision.

....

If you catch your man ogling a woman at a Christmas party, remember it's because women have wider peripheral vision and men have tunnel vision.

....

Because he was lacking in good peripheral vision, when Robert saw the attractive woman in the Santa suit, he had to turn his head to look. Sue, on the other hand, could easily see the woman in the Santa suit and the fact that Robert was looking at her.

In addition to their wide peripheral vision, women have better short-range vision than men, which means that they can spot an attractive woman before a man does. She'll make quick comparisons between herself and the potential competitor, usually negative ones against herself. When the man eventually spots her, he receives a negative reaction from his woman for ogling. A woman will usually have two negative thoughts in this situation: firstly, she mistakenly thinks that the man may prefer to be with the other woman than with her, and, secondly, that she is not as physically attractive as the other woman. Men are attracted visually to curves, leg lengths and shapes. Any woman with the right shape and proportions will catch his attention.

It doesn't mean that the man immediately wants to race the other woman off to bed, but it is a reminder to him that he is masculine and his evolutionary role is to look for opportunities to increase the size of the tribe. After all, he doesn't even know the other woman and could not realistically be thinking about a long-term relationship with her. This same principle applies to a man looking at the centrefold in a men's magazine, or eyeing up pictures of Girls Aloud in their sexy Christmas outfits. We are not making excuses for the rude, blatant ogling that some men do; we're simply explaining that if a man gets caught ogling at a Christmas party, it doesn't mean he doesn't love his partner – it's his biology at work. It's also interesting to note that in a public place like the beach or swimming pool, studies show that women ogle more than men. Being equipped with better peripheral vision, women rarely get caught.

Men are stimulated through their eyes, women through their ears. Men's brains are wired to look at female shapes and this is why erotic images have so much impact on them. Women, with their greater range of sensory information receptors, want to hear sweet words. A woman's sensitivity to hearing wonderful compliments is so strong, many women even close their eyes when their lover whispers sweet nothings.

What Men Need to Do

One of the best compliments a man can pay a woman is not to 'ogle' inappropriately at another female, particularly in public, but to give his partner a simultaneous compliment. For example, 'Sure, she's got great legs, but she's not in the same league as you, darling.' When this type of complimentary approach is used in the presence of other people, especially her friends, it pays big dividends to the man with the courage to try it. Women need to understand that a man is biologically compelled to look at certain female shapes and curves, and that they shouldn't feel threatened by it. An easy way for a woman to take the pressure off a man is for her to notice the other woman first and make the first comment. A man also needs to understand that no woman appreciates inappropriate ogling.

How to Improve Your Sex Life This Christmas

The person who first said that the way to a man's heart is through his stomach was aiming too high. After a man has had great sex, his softer, feminine side emerges. He can hear birds singing, is struck by the colours of the trees, can smell the flowers and is touched by the words of a song. Before sex, he probably only noticed the birds because of the mess they made on his car. But a man needs to understand that this after-sex side is the one that a woman loves to see and finds wonderfully seductive. If he can practise feeling this way, he'll be able to turn the woman on before having sex. At the same time, a woman needs to understand the importance of giving great sex to a man so she can glimpse this softer side and explain how alluring she finds it.

At the beginning of a new relationship, sex is always great and there is plenty of love. She gives him plenty of sex and he gives her plenty of love, and one thing feeds the other. After a few years, however, the man becomes preoccupied with lunch-chasing and the woman with nest-defending, which is why sex and love seem to stop simultaneously. Men and women are equally responsible for whether they have a good or bad sex life, but each often blames the other when things don't go well.

Men need to understand that a woman needs attention, praise, pampering and lots of time before she heats her electric oven. Women have to remember that these are the feelings men are more likely to express after a session of great sex. A man should remember how he felt after sex, and relive these feelings with a woman when he wants sex next time. A woman should be prepared to help him.

The key here is sex. For when sex is great, the whole relationship dramatically improves. So if you want to improve your relationship this Christmas, take a look at your sex life.

Why Sex Is Important at Christmas

There is an overwhelming amount of evidence that sex is great for your health. Having an amorous interlude an average of three times a week burns up 35,000 kilojoules, which is equal to running 130 kilometres in a year. Over the Christmas period, when many of us overindulge in fattening Christmas pudding and mince pies, this is obviously an added bonus. An average 100-gram portion of Christmas pudding contains a massive 330 calories and 11.8 grams of fat. And that doesn't include custard, cream or – God forbid – brandy butter. Along with a few glasses of wine and a glass of port, you can easily consume a day's calories at Christmas dinner. This may not sound too bad, but consider those Quality Street, the mince pies, turkey sandwich and champagne breakfast and the fact that most of us overindulge throughout the festive season, not just on Christmas Day, and you can see how easy it is to put on weight. Sex, as we all know, however, is very good at burning calories. The average person burns 120 to 180 calories in one half-hour session under the duvet.

*One mince pie with double cream roughly
equates to one hour of lovemaking.*

Sex also increases your testosterone levels, which fortify your bones and muscles and supply you with good cholesterol. Sex researcher Dr Beverley Whipple says, 'Endorphins, which are the body's natural painkillers, are released during sex and are good for relieving headache, whiplash and arthritis.'

*Sex has been proven to relieve headaches, so if you're suffering
from a Christmas hangover, sex could be the perfect solution.*

The hormone DHEA (dehydroepiandrosterone) is also released just prior to orgasm, and improves cognition, builds the immune system, inhibits tumour growth and builds bones. In a woman, oxytocin, the hormone that arouses the desire to be touched, is released in large doses during sex and her oestrogen levels also increase. Dr Harold Bloomfield, in his book *The Power of Five*, showed how oestrogen is associated with better bones and a better cardiovascular system in women. The effect of all these hormones is to protect the heart and extend life, so more sex equals longer life and less stress, which we know there is plenty of at Christmas.

All this means that sex is a great way of dealing with Christmas stress, to burn any extra calories you've consumed over the festive period and to make sure you're healthy for the year ahead. The list of benefits for having a vibrant sex life is getting longer and longer!

*Around 68 per cent of couples questioned in a poll by
Ann Summers said they planned to make up for any
festive sex drought by making love on New Year's Eve.*

Chapter 9

THE OFFICE CHRISTMAS PARTY

We've all heard plenty of stories of how people have made fools of themselves at the office Christmas party. For the most part, these stories are amusing and anecdotal, but it's true that the desire to let our hair down with colleagues after a year of hard work coupled with a little too much to drink can have a detrimental effect on other people's perception of us in the workplace and, consequently, our career. Inappropriate jokes, flirtations with colleagues and having to take a day off work due to overindulging in 'festive spirit' can all have a negative impact on how colleagues view us.

Two-thirds of photocopier-repair technicians at Canon report up to a 25 per cent increase in call-outs over Christmas in the United Kingdom due to photocopier-related mishaps. An astonishing 32 per cent of their service calls at this time of year are 'to repair copier glass that had been sat on' or 'to fix paper jams that revealed evidence of embarrassing images'.

What's more, in a survey of 1,200 British office workers, researchers found that almost half recalled dirty dancing, one-third had kissed a co-worker (with or without the mistletoe), and a quarter confessed to extravagant behaviour, if not exhibitionism. Incredibly, 20 per cent said that they had spoken angrily to the boss. Even more worryingly, there has been a marked rise in the number of complaints of discrimination and harassment at Christmas parties in recent years, and many employers are now steering clear of holding festive parties at all for fear of law suits. According to one survey, three out of four bosses said that a member of their staff has threatened to take a case to an employment tribunal following bad behaviour at a Christmas party.

'Christmas is a time when everybody wants his past forgotten and his present remembered. What I don't like about office Christmas parties is looking for a job the next day.'
PHYLLIS DILLER

Most people understand that how we interact socially with work colleagues can have a huge impact on the success of our career. We are far more likely to be seen as a 'team-player' and as outgoing and approachable if we are seen to get on well with colleagues. But few people consider the huge impact that the office Christmas party can have on their careers.

Making a success of the Christmas party isn't just about avoiding drinking too much and watching what you say – it can be the perfect opportunity to network and improve other people's perception of you in the workplace, and can also be a chance for you to assess your colleagues and study their body language. Handled correctly, the office Christmas party can further your career, not ruin it. This doesn't mean that you can't enjoy yourself. It is Christmas, after all! In this chapter, we will outline the top four ways in which body language can be used to influence people and improve your colleagues' view of you. The four areas we will look at are:

1 Handshakes
2 Standing
3 Mirroring
4 Smiling

1 Handshakes: How to Make a Good First Impression

At an office Christmas party or other work function, you are likely to be introduced to numerous people with whom you will have to shake hands. The way you greet fellow party-goers can have a huge impact on how you are received and what they think of you. The hands have been the most important tools in human evolution, and there are more connections between the brain and the hands than between any other body parts. Few people ever consider how their hands behave or the way they shake hands when they meet someone. Yet those first five to seven pumps establish whether dominance, submission or power plays will take place.

Shaking hands is a relic of our ancient past. Whenever primitive tribes met under friendly conditions, they would hold their arms out with their palms exposed to show that no weapons were being held or concealed. In Roman times, the practice of carrying a concealed dagger in the sleeve was common, so for protection the Romans developed the Lower-Arm-Grasp – in which both parties grasp each other's wrist rather than the hand – as a common greeting.

The modern form of this ancient greeting ritual is the interlocking and shaking of the palms and was originally used in the nineteenth century to seal commercial trans-actions between men of equal status. It has become wide-spread only in the last hundred years or so and has always remained in the male domain until recent times. In most Western and European countries today, it is performed both on initial greeting and on departure in all business contexts, and increasingly at parties and social events by both women and men.

The handshake evolved as a way men could cement a commercial deal with each other.

How Dominance and Control Are Communicated

In Roman times, two leaders would meet and greet each other with what amounted to a standing version of modern arm-wrestling. If one leader was stronger than the other, his hand would finish above the other's hand in what became known as the Upper-Hand position.

Let's assume that you are at the office Christmas party and have just been introduced to a colleague whom you have not met before and you greet each other with a handshake. One of three basic attitudes is subconsciously transmitted:

1 Dominance: 'He is trying to dominate me. I'd better be cautious.'
2 Submission: 'I can dominate this person. He'll do what I want.'
3 Equality: 'I feel comfortable with this person.'

These attitudes are sent and received without our being aware of them, but they can have an immediate and dramatic impact.

The Dominant Handshake

Dominance is transmitted by turning your hand so that your palm faces down in the handshake. Your palm doesn't have to face directly down, but is the upper hand and communicates that you want to take control of the encounter.

Our study of 350 successful senior management executives (89 per cent of whom were men) revealed that not only did almost all of the managers initiate the handshake, 88 per cent of males and 31 per cent of females also used the dominant handshake position. Power and control issues are generally less important to women, which probably accounts for why only one in three women attempted the Upper-Hand ritual.

We also found that some women will give men a soft handshake in some social contexts to imply submissiveness. This is a way of highlighting their femininity or implying that domination of her may be possible. The office Christmas party is partly a social setting, but it should still be considered a business context: women should avoid giving men a soft handshake at an office party because men will give attention to her feminine qualities and not take her seriously. Women who display high femininity in business are not taken seriously by other business women or men, despite the fact that it's now fashionable or politically correct to say everyone is the same. This doesn't mean a woman in business needs to act in a masculine way; she simply needs to avoid signals of femaleness such as soft handshakes, short skirts and high heels if she wants equal credibility.

The office Christmas party is ostensibly a social setting, but if you want to get ahead, you should take care to give a good impression.

In 2001, William Chaplin at the University of Alabama conducted a study into handshakes and found that extroverted types use firm handshakes, while shy, neurotic personalities don't. Chaplin also found that women who are open to new ideas used firm handshakes. Men used the same handshakes whether they were open to new ideas or not. So it makes good business sense for women to practise firmer handshaking, particularly with men.

The Submissive Handshake

The opposite of the dominant handshake is to offer your hand with your palm facing upwards, symbolically giving the other person the upper hand, like a dog exposing its throat to a superior dog. This can be effective if you want to give the other person control or allow him to feel that he is in charge of the situation.

While the palm-up handshake can communicate a submissive attitude, there are sometimes other circumstances to consider. For instance, a person with arthritis in their hands will be forced to give you a limp handshake because of their condition and this makes it easy to turn their palm into the submissive position. People who use their hands in their profession, such as surgeons, artists and musicians, may also give a limp handshake, purely to protect their hands. The gesture clusters they use following their handshake will give further clues for your assessment of them – a submissive person will use more submissive gestures, and a dominant person will use more assertive gestures.

The Equal Handshake

When two dominant people shake hands, a symbolic power struggle takes place as each person attempts to turn the other's palm into the submissive position. The result is a vice-like handshake with both palms remaining in the vertical position and this creates a feeling of equality and mutual respect because neither is prepared to give in to the other. This might take place at a Christmas party if you are shaking hands with someone who is the same level as you.

How to Create Rapport

It is particularly important to try to create rapport in a handshake at the Christmas party, because this is after all partly a social setting – a chance to bond and network. There are two key ingredients for creating rapport. First, make sure that yours and the other person's palms are in the vertical position so that no one is dominant or submissive. Second, apply the same pressure you receive. This means that if, on a firmness scale of one to ten, your handshake registers a seven but the other person is only a five, you'll need to back off 20 per cent in strength. If their grip is a nine and yours is a seven, you'll need to increase your grip by 20 per cent.

If you are meeting a group of people, you'd probably need to make several adjustments of angle and intensity to create a feeling of rapport with everyone and to stay on an equal footing with each person – so if you are being introduced to lots of different people at the Christmas party, make sure you vary your handshake. Also keep in mind that the average male hand can exert around twice the power of the average female hand, so allowances must be made for this. Remember that the handshake always needs to be warm, friendly and positive.

When Men and Women Shake Hands

Even though women have had a strong presence in the work-force for several decades, many men and women still experience degrees of fumbling and embarrassment in male-female greetings. This may happen at the office Christmas party if one of you is unsure whether you should shake hands or greet each other less formally. Most men report that they received some basic handshaking training from their fathers when they were boys, but few women report the same training. As adults, this can create uncomfortable situations when a man reaches first to shake a woman's hand but she may not see it – she's initially more intent on looking at his face. Feeling awkward with his hand suspended in mid-air, the man pulls it back hoping she didn't notice, but as he does, she reaches for it and is also left with her hand dangling in a void. He reaches for her hand again and the result is a mish-mash of tangled fingers that look and feel like two eager squid in a love embrace.

If this does happen to you at the party, intentionally take the other person's right hand with your left, place it correctly into your right hand and say with a smile, 'Let's try that again!' This can give you an enormous credibility boost with the other person, because it shows you care enough about meeting them to get the handshake right. If you are a woman in business, a wise strategy is to hold your hand out as early as possible to give clear notice of your intention to shake hands and this will avoid any fumbling.

The Cold, Clammy Handshake

Apart from gripping too hard, one of the worst handshakes you can give at the office Christmas party is the cold, clammy handshake. If we become tense when meeting strangers or at parties, blood diverts away from the cells below the outer layer of the skin on the hands – known as the dermis – and goes to the arm and leg muscles for 'fight or flight' preparation. The result is that our hands lose temperature and begin to sweat, making them feel cold and clammy and resulting in a handshake that feels like a wet salmon.

The palms have more sweat glands than any other part of the body, which is why sweaty palms become so obvious. If it's possible to do so, nip to the restroom or quickly and discreetly dry your palms on a napkin before meeting someone important.

Perfecting your handshake at the office Christmas party: keep the palms held vertical and match the other person's grip for a $^{10}/_{10}$ handshake.

2   Standing: How to Convey Openness and Approachability

How you stand and hold yourself at the office Christmas party will have a huge impact on how others perceive you – do you look at ease but still professional, or do you look nervous and unapproachable?

Avoid Folded and Crossed Arms

No matter how nervous you feel at the party, or how anxious you are about meeting new people and socialising, folded and crossed arms must be avoided at all times. Hiding behind a barrier is a normal response we learn at an early age to protect ourselves. As children, we hid behind solid objects such as tables, chairs, furniture and Mother's skirt whenever we found ourselves in a threatening situation. As we grow older, the arm-crossing gesture can be less obvious to others, but is still an unconscious attempt to block out what we perceive as a threat or undesirable circumstances. The arms fold neatly across the heart and lungs region to protect these vital organs from being injured, so it's likely that arm-crossing is inborn. One thing's certain: when a person has a nervous, negative or defensive attitude, it's very likely he will fold his arms firmly on his chest, showing that he feels threatened.

Rather than take a full Arm-Cross gesture, which can tell everyone we are fearful, women often substitute a subtler version – a Partial-Arm-Cross, where one arm swings across the body to hold or touch the other arm to form the barrier and it looks as if she is hugging herself.

Men use a partial arm barrier known as Holding-Hands-With-Yourself – the hands are clasped together in front of the man's groin. Also known as the Broken-Zipper position, it makes a man feel secure because he can protect his 'crown jewels' and can avoid the consequences of receiving a nasty frontal blow.

At the Christmas party, the most common version of creating a subtle barrier is to hold a glass or cup with two hands. You need only one hand to hold a glass, but two hands allows the insecure person to form an almost unnoticeable arm barrier. If you want people to think you are comfortable and open, only hold your glass with one hand.

If you want to create a good impression at the office Christmas party, do *not* stand with your arms crossed or with one or both folded across the chest – you may feel 'comfortable' like this, but studies have shown that other people's reactions to these gestures is negative – others will assume you are not approachable or are unwilling to participate.

The Boss vs the Staff

At the office Christmas party, it is likely that staff members of different levels will meet and talk to each other. Status can influence arm-folding gestures, so the way you hold yourself can be revelatory.

A superior type can make his superiority felt by not folding his arms, saying, in effect, 'I'm not afraid, so I'll keep my body open and vulnerable.' Let's say, for example, that at the company Christmas party, the general manager is introduced to several new employees. Having greeted them with a Palm-Down handshake, he stands back from them – a metre away – with his hands by his side or behind his back in the way Prince Philip stands, with one palm held loosely in the other (superiority), or with one or both hands in his pocket (non-involvement). He rarely folds his arms across his chest so as not to show the slightest hint of nervousness.

Conversely, after shaking hands with the boss, the new employees may take full or partial arm-crossing positions because of their apprehension about being in the presence of the company's top person or they may clasp their glasses with two hands. Both the general manager and the new employees feel comfortable with their respective gesture clusters as each is signalling his status, relative to the other. But what happens when the general manager meets a young, up-and-coming male who is also a superior type and who may even signal that he is as important as the general manager? The likely outcome is that after the two give each other a dominant handshake, the younger executive may take an arm-fold gesture with both thumbs pointing upwards.

The Thumbs-Up gesture is a way of showing others we have a self-confident attitude, and the folded arms still give a feeling of protection. It is a useful one to remember if you want to convey a positive, confident demeanour.

The Main Standing Positions

How we position our legs also plays a role in how others will perceive us at the office party. The next time you attend a party you will notice some groups of people standing with their arms and legs crossed. Look more closely and you'll also see that they are standing at a greater distance from each other than the customary social distance.

If they are wearing coats or jackets, they are likely to be buttoned. This is how most people stand when they are among people whom they don't know well. If you interact with them you would find that one or all of them are unfamiliar with others in the group.

While open legs can show openness or dominance, crossed legs shows a closed, submissive or defensive attitude as they symbolically deny any access to the genitals.

Imagine now that you notice another group of people standing with arms unfolded, palms visible, coats unbuttoned, relaxed appearance and leaning back on one leg with the other pointing towards others in the group. All are gesturing with their hands and moving in and out of each other's personal space. Closer investigation would reveal that these people are friends or are known personally to each other. The first group of people with the closed arms and legs may have relaxed facial expressions and conversation that sounds free and easy, but the folded arms and legs tell us that they are not as relaxed or confident with each other as they are trying to appear.

If you were to join this group and stand with your arms and legs tightly crossed and wear a serious expression, one by one the other group members will cross their arms and legs and remain in that position until you, the stranger, leave – at which point the members of the group will gradually assume their original open poses once again.

Crossing the legs not only reveals negative or defensive emotions, it makes a person appear insecure and causes others to react accordingly.

How to Look Relaxed

As people begin to feel more comfortable in a group and get to know others, they move through a series of movements taking them from the defensive crossed arms and legs position to the relaxed open position. This standing 'opening-up' procedure follows the same sequence everywhere.

It begins with the closed position, arms and legs crossed. As they begin to feel comfortable with each other and rapport builds, their legs uncross first and their feet are placed together in the Attention position. Next, the arm folded on top in the Arm-Cross comes out and the palm is occasionally flashed when speaking but is eventually not used as a barrier. Instead, it may hold the outside of the other arm in a Single-Arm Barrier. Both arms unfold next, and one arm gestures or may be placed on the hip or in the pocket. Finally, one person takes the Foot-Forward position, showing acceptance of the other person.

If you want people to think you are comfortable and confident at the office Christmas party, assume an open position. If your standing position is relaxed and open, other people will respond accordingly.

Perfecting your stance at the office Christmas party:
to convey approachability and confidence, assume an open
stance. Do not fold or cross your arms, or grip your glass
with two hands. If your standing position is relaxed and
open, other people will respond accordingly.

---

3 Mirroring: How to Build Rapport

Mirroring other people's body language at the Christmas party is an excellent way of building rapport, provided it is done subtly.

When we meet others for the first time, we need to assess quickly whether they are positive or negative towards us, just as most other animals do for survival reasons. We do this by scanning the other person's body to see if they will move or gesture the same way we do in what is known as 'mirroring'. We mirror each other's body language as a way of bonding, being accepted and creating rapport, but we are usually oblivious to the fact that we are doing it. In ancient times, mirroring was a social device that helped our ancestors fit in successfully with larger groups; it is also a left-over from a primitive method of learning which involved imitation.

Non-verbally, mirroring says, 'Look at me; I'm the same as you. I feel the same way and share the same attitudes.' This is why people at a rock concert will all jump to their feet and applaud simultaneously or give a 'Mexican Wave' together. The synchronicity of the crowd promotes a secure feeling in the participants.

Mirroring makes others feel 'at ease'. It's such a powerful rapport-building tool that slow-motion video research reveals that it even extends to simultaneous blinking, nostril-flaring, eyebrow-raising and even pupil dilation, which is remarkable as these micro-gestures cannot be consciously imitated.

Mirroring Differences Between Men and Women

The most important technique that men can use to build rapport at the office Christmas party is to subtly mirror women's expressions when listening.

Geoffrey Beattie, at the University of Manchester, found that a woman is instinctively four times more likely to mirror another woman than a man is to mirror another man. He also found that women mirror men's body language too, but

men are reluctant to mirror a woman's gestures or posture –
unless he is in courtship mode.

....

Men can use mirroring to good effect to build
rapport with female colleagues at Christmas functions.

....

When a woman says she can 'see' that someone doesn't agree
with the group opinion she is actually 'seeing' the disagreement. She's picked up that someone's body language is out of
sync with group opinion and they are showing their disagreement by not mirroring the group's body language. Men's
brains are simply not well equipped to read the fine detail of
other people's body language and don't consciously notice
mirroring discrepancies.

Typically, a woman can use an average of six main facial
expressions in a ten-second listening period to reflect and
then feed-back the speaker's emotions. Her face will mirror
the emotions being expressed by the speaker. Men, on the
other hand, can make fewer than a third of the facial expressions a woman can make. Men usually hold expressionless
faces, especially in public, because of the evolutionary need
to withhold emotion to stave off possible attack from strangers
and to appear to be in control of their emotions.

A woman reads the meaning of what is being said through
the speaker's voice tone and his emotional condition through
his body language. This is exactly what a man needs to do to
keep a woman interested and listening. Most men are daunt-
ed by the prospect of using facial feedback while listening,
but it pays big dividends for the man who becomes good at it.

What to Do About It If You're Female

The key to mirroring a man's behaviour is in understanding
that he doesn't use his face to signal his attitudes – he uses his
body. Most women find it difficult to mirror an expressionless man, but with males this is not required. If you're a

woman, it means that you need to reduce your facial expressions so that you don't come across as overwhelming or intimidating. Most importantly, don't mirror what you think he might be feeling. That can be disastrous if you've got it wrong and you may be described as 'dizzy' or 'scatterbrained'. Women in business who listen with a more serious face are described by men as more intelligent, astute and sensible.

Intentionally Creating Rapport

The significance of mirroring is one of the most important body language lessons you can learn because it's a clear way in which others tell us that they agree with us or like us. It is also a way for us to tell others that we like them, by simply mirroring their body language.

At the office Christmas party, if a boss wants to develop a rapport and create a relaxed atmosphere with a nervous employee, he could copy the employee's posture to achieve this end. Similarly, an up-and-coming employee may be seen copying his boss's gestures in an attempt to show agreement when the boss is giving his opinion. Using this knowledge, it is possible to influence others by mirroring their positive gestures and posture. This has the effect of putting the other person in a receptive and relaxed frame of mind, because he can 'see' that you understand his point of view.

Research shows that when the leader of a group assumes certain gestures and positions, subordinates will copy, usually in pecking order. At an office Christmas party, leaders tend to be the first of a group to instigate an action – they may, for instance, be the first to eat from the buffet, or if there are Christmas crackers at a meal, be the first to initiate, and they like to sit on the end of a sofa, table or bench seat rather than in the centre.

Before you mirror someone's body language, however, you must take into consideration your relationship with that person. If a senior manager is sitting on a desk at the office Christmas party or assuming a macho Crotch Display, showing the employee a superior, dominant attitude, it would be inappropriate for a very junior employee to mirror these gestures. The manager could feel affronted by the employee's body language.

Mirroring is effective for intimidating or disarming 'superior' types who try to take control. By mirroring, you can disconcert them and force a change of position. But never do it to the boss, and never mirror someone's inappropriate antics at the Christmas party!

....

Perfecting mirroring at the Christmas party: when you are talking to someone, mirror his seating position, posture, body angle, gestures, expressions and tone of voice. Before long, they'll start to feel that there's something about you they like – they'll describe you as 'easy to be with'. This is because they see themselves reflected in you. A word of warning, however: don't do it too much or too obviously.

....

4   Smiling: How to Make People Like You

Children were often told by their grandmothers to 'put on a happy face', 'wear a big smile' and 'show your pearly whites' when meeting someone new because Grandma knew, on an intuitive level, it would produce a positive reaction in others. Smiling is one of the most powerful things you can do at the office Christmas party to influence people and make them like you. In Chapter 6, we learned a little about how contagious smiling is. Now we'll look at how fake smiling can help influence your colleagues.

Why You Should Laugh at Your Boss's Jokes

Professor Ulf Dimberg at Uppsala University, Sweden, conducted an experiment that revealed how your unconscious mind exerts direct control of your facial muscles. Using equipment that picks up electrical signals from muscle fibres, he measured the facial muscle activity on 120 volunteers while they were exposed to pictures of both happy and angry faces. They were told to make frowning, smiling or expressionless faces in response to what they saw. Sometimes the face they were told to attempt was the opposite of what they saw – meeting a smile with a frown, or a frown with a smile. The results showed that the volunteers did not have total control over their facial muscles. While it was easy to frown back at a picture of an angry man, it was much more difficult to pull a smile. Even though volunteers were trying consciously to control their natural reactions, the twitching in their facial muscles told a different story – they were mirroring the expressions they were seeing, even when they were trying not to.

This is why regular smiling is important to have as a part of your body language repertoire, even when you don't feel like it – such as when your boss is telling you a terrible joke – because smiling directly influences other people's attitudes and how they respond to you.

....

Science has proved that the more you smile, the more positive reactions others will give you, so laughing at your boss's jokes at the office Christmas party really is worth the effort!

....

Smiles and Laughter Are a Way of Bonding

Robert Provine found that laughing was more than 30 times as likely to occur in participants in a social situation than in a solitary setting. Laughter, he found, has less to do with jokes and funny stories and more to do with building relationships. He found that only 15 per cent of our laughter has to do with jokes. In Provine's studies, participants were more likely to speak to themselves when alone than they were to laugh. Participants were videotaped watching a humorous video clip in three different situations: alone, with a same-sex stranger and with a same-sex friend.

....

Only 15 per cent of our laughter has to do with jokes. Laughter has more to do with bonding.

....

Even though no differences existed between how funny the participants felt the video clip was, those who watched the amusing video clips alone laughed significantly less than did those who watched the video clip with another person present, whether it was a friend or a stranger. The frequency and time spent laughing were significantly greater in both situations involving another person than when the participant was alone. Laughter occurred much more frequently during social interaction. These results demonstrate that the more social a situation is, the more often people will laugh and the longer each laugh will last.

Smiling Advice for Women

A word of advice for women at the office Christmas party. Research by Marvin Hecht and Marianne La France from Boston University has revealed how subordinate people smile more in the presence of dominant and superior people, in both friendly and unfriendly situations, whereas superior people will smile only around subordinate people in friendly situations.

This research shows that women smile far more than men in both social and business situations, which can make a woman appear to be subordinate or weak in an encounter with unsmiling men. The likely explanation for women's extra smiling is that smiling fits neatly into women's evolutionary role as pacifiers and nurturers. It doesn't mean a woman can't be as authoritative as a man; but the extra smiling can make her look less authoritative.

Social psychologist Dr Nancy Henley, at UCLA, described a woman's smile as 'her badge of appeasement' and it is often used to placate a more powerful male. Her research showed that, in social encounters, women smile 87 per cent of the time versus 67 per cent for men and that women are 26 per cent more likely to return smiles from the opposite sex. Pictures of unsmiling women were decoded as a sign of unhappiness, while pictures of unsmiling men were seen as a sign of dominance.

The lessons here are for women to smile less when dealing with dominant men in business, such as at the Christmas party, or to mirror the amount of smiling that men do. And if men want to be more persuasive with women, they need to smile more in all contexts.

....

Perfecting smiling at the office Christmas party: laughter and smiling are a very important part of bonding. Men should try to smile more if they want people to respond well to them; women should avoid smiling too much if they want to appear to be strong and in control.

....

Summary: How to Be a Hit at the Office Christmas Party

The first rule of being a success at the office Christmas party is to avoid drinking too much – it could leave you with regrets as well as a hangover. Remember that once the party's over you have to go back to work. Alcohol is well known to be a disinhibitor. It is easy to be tempted to say too much, give personal details about yourself that you'd rather were kept private or voice an opinion about a colleague that you wish you'd kept to yourself. If you need an excuse for not drinking, you might consider saying that you need to drive, if that is appropriate for your circumstances. Co-workers won't forget the impression you have left: even if you can't remember what happened, they will!

The office Christmas party is a prime opportunity to meet

new people, develop relationships and build rapport with colleagues. You should have fun, but remember that the Christmas party is just as important as any other work function. The body language skills we have taught you in this chapter will help you to make a good, lasting impression on co-workers and superiors, and to establish how other people see themselves in the office hierarchy.

Remember, networking and socialising with colleagues are key aspects of building a successful career. Follow our advice and you could make this Christmas party one to remember, for all the right reasons.

CONCLUSION

Your mother's yearly meltdown that the turkey isn't cooking quickly enough or is going to be dry, battling over the remote control while complaining that yet again there is nothing good on the television, groaning at notoriously bad Christmas-cracker jokes . . . Much as Christmas may be stressful, and busy, and challenging, we would miss it if we didn't celebrate it. According to a *Guardian*/ICM poll, 94 per cent of Brits celebrate Christmas, regardless of their faith. In spite of all the planning, family feuds, commercialism, battling between the sexes and money worries, 75 per cent of people agreed with the statement 'If the truth were to be told, I love Christmas.'

Why We Love Christmas

Because a large part of this book has focused on the differences between men and women and the difficulties this can cause at Christmas, you could be forgiven for thinking that our own attitude towards Christmas is a little 'Bah, humbug.' On the contrary, we love Christmas. We, the authors, are happily married, faithful lovers and best friends. We are also the parents of four beautiful children. Together, we have enjoyed many happy Christmases. But we also know the potential pitfalls and disaster areas that can cause problems between couples. In this book, we have drawn on our personal experience as well as research and feel we have given you a balanced view of relationships at Christmas from many different points of view and, hopefully, without bias. Writing and researching our books has given us a greater understanding of each other, our parents, brothers, sisters, cousins, co-workers and neighbours – and it's only through understanding each other that we can really enjoy Christmas in spite of all our differences and peculiarities. We don't always get it right, but feel we do most of the time with most people. As a result, we are rarely in an argument with anyone close to us and they all love us for it. It's not always perfect, but regularly, it is.

Mr and Mrs Santa Claus

It's great to be a man at Christmas because you get to play with your kid's new train set, there's always a Bond film on TV and you have a legitimate excuse for looking at photos of Kylie in her sexy Santa outfit. It's great to be a woman at Christmas because it's the one time in the year when you can eat as much chocolate as you want, you know no one will buy you novelty socks as a present and the sales give you the perfect opportunity to spend all day at the shopping centre.

Maybe one day men and women will be like each other. Maybe women will ask for a new table saw for Christmas and hope that the Christmas movie has got guns and gore in it. Maybe men will do their Christmas shopping in plenty of time and will offer to wrap all the Christmas presents. We doubt it – at least, not for a few thousand Christmases. Meanwhile, we'll continue to understand, manage and learn to love our differences. The result will be a happier, more peaceful Christmas for your whole family.

How to Give This Book as a Christmas Present

Following the worldwide success of our books *Why Men Don't Listen & Women Can't Read Maps* and *Why Men Don't Have a Clue & Women Always Need More Shoes*, some men accused us of making their lives difficult. They felt their women were using our book to persecute them by saying, 'Allan said this . . .' or, 'Barbara said that . . .' Our books are a favourite of women everywhere and we are aware that some did give them to the males in their lives with the comment 'You need this! Read it from cover to cover – in fact, I've highlighted the parts you need to read.'

If you're a woman and are planning on giving this book to a man as a Christmas present, or as any kind of gift, we have a few words of advice. When a woman gives a personal-development book to another woman, the woman who receives it is honoured and thankful for a gift that may help her improve. A man, however, may feel insulted and feel the woman is saying he's not good enough the way he is. 'I don't need this!' he'll say dismissively as he hands it back to her, leaving her feeling hurt and upset.

So, if you're a man reading this, you're part of a minority who want to get a handle on how women think and behave – congratulations! If you're a woman, it could be safer to buy it for yourself for Christmas and ask a man his opinion on the book's advice because, as we know, men love to give opinions. Highlight the pages you want him to read and leave the book on the coffee table or in the toilet. Or buy him a ticket for one of our relationship seminars.

Why Christmas Is Good for You

In Chapter 6, we saw that laughter can be beneficial for you and has a knock-on effect on those around you. Christmas is a time for fun and enjoyment. Take time to enjoy the festive season – in all likelihood, no one will remember if your Christmas crackers were homemade or if you were up until two on Christmas Eve making your own canapés. Everyone will remember, though, that you looked happy and relaxed and they will have a better time because of it.

....

Even Christmas dinner can be good for you if you make the right choices – turkey is a very low-fat option, all those Brussels sprouts contribute to your recommended five-a-day, cranberry sauce is packed with antioxidants, and alcohol in moderation cuts the risk of heart disease.

....

Christmas is the one time of year when you can really let your hair down. It brings neighbours, colleagues and families closer together, and it gives us a chance to show those we love just how much we care. We firmly believe that using the tools offered in *Why He's So Last Minute & She's Got It All Wrapped Up* can help all men and women have a happier, more fulfilling and sexier Christmas. We want you to have the best Christmas possible and we hope that, with the advice we've given you in these pages, this Christmas will be your happiest yet. We hope you have enjoyed reading our book and we wish you a very Merry Christmas!

REFERENCES

Acredolo, L. and Goodwin, S., *Baby Signs: How to Talk with Your Baby Before Your Baby Can Talk*, Vermilion (2000)

Acton, G. S., 'Measurement of impulsivity in a hierarchical model of personality traits: implications for substance use', *Substance Use and Abuse*, in press (2003)

Adams, R. S., Biddle, B. and Holt, *Realities of Teaching: Exploration with Video Tape*, Rinehart & Winston (1970)

Alder, Harry, *NLP in 21 Days*, Piatkus (1999)

Allen, L. S., Richey, M. F., Chai, Y. M. and Gorski, R. A., 'Sex differences in the corpus callosum of the living human being', *Journal of Neuroscience*, 11, 933–42 (1991)

Allen and Gorski, 'Sexual orientation and the size of the anterior commissure in the human brain', *Proceedings of the National Academy of Sciences*, 89, 7199–202 (1992)

Amen, Daniel G., *Change Your Brain, Change Your Life: The Breakthrough Program for Conquering Anxiety, Depression, Obsessiveness, Anger and Impulsiveness*, Times Books (2000)

Andreas, S. and Faulkner, C., *NLP: The New Technology of Achievement*, Nicholas Brealey Publishing (1996)

Andrews, Simon, *Anatomy of Desire: The Science and Psychology of Sex, Love and Marriage*, Little, Brown (2000)

Antes, J. R., McBridge, R. B. and Collins, J. D., 'The effect of a new city route on the cognitive maps of its residents', *Environment and Behaviour*, 20, 75–91 (1988)

Aquinas, Thomas, *Summa Theologica*, translated by the Fathers of the English Dominican Province, Burnes, Oates & Washburn (1922) [Distinguishes between the degrees of turpitude of various kinds of lie.]

Archer, John and Lloyd Barbara, *Sex and Gender*, Cambridge University Press (1995)

Ardrey, R., *The Territorial Imperative*, Collins (1967)

Argyle, M. and Cook, M., *Gaze and Mutual Gaze*, Cambridge University Press (1976)

Argyle, *Bodily Communication*, Methuen (1975)

Argyle, 'The syntax of bodily communication', *Linguistics*, 112, 71–91 (1973)

Argyle, *Skills with People: A Guide for Managers*, Hutchinson (1973)

Argyle and Ingham, R., 'Gaze, mutual gaze and proximity', *Semiotica*, 6, 32–49 (1972)

Argyle, *Social Interaction*, Methuen (1968)

Argyle, *The Psychology of Interpersonal Behaviour*, Penguin Books (1967)

Argyle, *Training Manager*, The Acton Society Trust, London (1962)

Arons, Harry, *Hypnosis in Criminal Investigation*, Charles C. Thomas (1967)

Asher, M., *Body Language*, Carlton, 1999

Augustine, 'Lying' and 'Against Lying', in *Treatises on Various Subjects*, R. J. Deferrari (ed.), Catholic University of America Press (1952)
[Early and highly influential prohibition against all forms of lying.]

Axtell, R. E., *Gestures*, John Wiley & Sons (1991)

Bacon, A. M., *A Manual of Gestures*, Griggs, Chicago (1875)

Bailey, F. Lee, *For the Defense*, The New American Library, Inc. (1976)

Bailey and Aronson, H., *The Defense Never Rests*, Signet (1972)

Baker, Robin, *Sperm Wars: Infidelity, Sexual Conflict and other Bedroom Battles*, Fourth Estate, Allen & Unwin (1997)

Bandler, R. and Grinder, J., *Patterns of the Hypnotic Techniques of Milton H. Erickson, MD*, Vol. 1, Metamorphous Press (1997)

Bandler, R., *Insider's Guide to Sub-modalities*, Meta Publications (1993)

Bandler and Grinder, *Frogs into Princes: Neuro-Linguistic Programming*, Real People Press, Moab, Utah (1979)

Bandler and Grinder, *The Structure of Magic: A Book About Language and Therapy*, Science and Behavior Books (1976)

Barash, D., *Sociobiology*, Fontana (1981)

Barkow, J., Cossmides, L. and Tooby, J., *The Adapted Mind: Evolutionary Psychology and the Generation of Culture*, Oxford University Press (1992)

Barry, Dave, *Dave Barry's Complete Guide to Guys*, Ballatine Publishing Group (2000)

Bart, Dr Benjamin, *The History of Farting*, Heron (1993)

Baum, M. J., Bressler, S. C., Daum, M. C., Veiga, C. A. and McNamee, C. S., 'Ferret mothers provide more anogental licking to male offspring: possible contribution to psychosexual differentiation', *Physiology and Behaviour*, 60, 353–9 (1996)

Beattie, G., *Visible Thought: The New Psychology of Body Language* (2003)

Beattie, *All Talk: Why It's Important to Watch your Words and Everything Else you Say*, Weidenfeld & Nicolson, London (1988)

Beattie, *The Candarel Guide to Beach Watching*, Hove, Rambletree (1988)

Beatty, W. W., 'The Fargo map test: a standardised method for assessing remote memory for visuospatial information', *Journal of Clinical Psychology*, 44, 61–7 (1988)

Beatty and Truster, A. I., 'Gender differences in geographical knowledge', *Sex Roles*, 16, 565–90 (1987)

Becker, Jill B., *Behavioural Endocrinology*, MIT Press (1992)

Belli, Melvin, *My Life on Trial*, Popular Library (1977)

Benbow, C. P. and Stanley, J. C., 'Sex differences in mathematical reasoning ability: more facts', *Science*, 222, 1029–31 (1983)

Benthall, J. and Polhemus, T., *The Body As a Medium of Expression*, Allen Lane, London (1975)

Berenbaum, S. A. K. and Leveroni, C., 'Early hormones and sex differences in cognitive abilities', *Learning and Individual Differences*, 7, 303–21 (1995)

Berenbaum, 'Psychological Outcome in Congenital Adrenal Hyperplasia', in *Therapeutic Outcome of Endocrine Disorders: Efficacy, Innovation and Quality of Life*, B. Stabler and B. B. Bercy (eds), 186–99, Springer (2000)

Berne, E., *Games People Play*, Grove Press, New York (1964)

Berrebi, A. S. et al., 'Corpus callosum: region-specific effects of sex, early experience and age', *Brain Research*, 438, 216–24 (1988)

Berry, J. W., 'Ecological and social factors in spatial perceptual development', *Canadian Journal of Behavioural Science*, 3, 324–36 (1971)

Berry, 'Temne and Eskimo perceptual skills', *International Journal of Psychology*, 1, 207–29 (1966)

Biddulph, Steve and Shaaron, *More Secrets of Happy Children*, HarperCollins (1994)

Biddulph, Steve, *Raising Boys*, Celestial Arts, Berkeley (1998)

Birdwhistell, R. L., 'The language of the body: the natural environment of words' in A. Silverstein (ed.) *Human Communication: Theoretical Explorations*, 203–20, Lawrence, Hillsdale, New Jersey (1974)

Birdwhistell, R. L., *Kinesics and Context*, Allen Lane, London (1971)

Birdwhistell, *Introduction to Kinesics*, University of Louisville Press (1952)

Black, H., 'Amygdala's inner workings', *The Scientist*, 15 (19), 20 (1 October 2001)

Blacking, J., *Anthropology of the Body*, Academic Press, London/New York (1977)

Block, Eugene B., *Voice Printing: How the Law Can Read the Voice of Crime*, Veronica School District 47J, Petitioner v. Wayne Action et ux, Guardians ad Litem for JAMES ACTON 515 US —, 132L Ed 2d 564,

115 S Ct — |No 94–590| US Supreme Court Reports, 132 L Ed (Drug Abuse Screening by Urinalysis Decision.) Argued 28 March 1995. Decided 26 June 1995

Blum, Deborah, *Sex on the Brain*, Viking/Penguin (1997)

Bok, S., *Lying: Moral Choice in Public and Private Life*, Pantheon (1978)

Booth, A. et al., 'The influence of testosterone on deviance in adulthood: assessing and explaining the relationship', *Criminology*, Vol. 31 (1), 93–117 (1 November 1993)

Botting, Kate and Douglas, *Sex Appeal*, Boxtree (1995)

Bottomley, M., *Executive Image*, Penguin (1988)

Boyd, R. and Silk J. R., *How Humans Evolved*, Norton, New York (1996)

Brasch, R., *How Did Sex Begin?*, David McKay (1997)

Brown, M. A. and M. J. Broadway, 'The cognitive maps of adolescents: confusion about inter-town distances', *Professional Geographer*, 33, 315–25 (1981)

Brun, T., *The International Dictionary of Sign Language*, Wolfe Publishing, London (1969)

Bryan, W. J., *The Psychology of Jury Selection*, Vantage Press, New York (1971)

Budesheim, T. L. and Depaola, S. J., 'Beauty or the beast? The effects of appearance, personality, and issue information on evaluations of political candidates', *Personality and Social Psychology Bulletin*, 20, 339–48 (1994)

Burr, C. I., *A Separate Creation*, Bantam Press, 167–77 (1996)

Burton, S., *Impostors: Six Kinds of Liar*, Viking (2000)

Buss, D., *The Evolution of Desire*, Basic Books/HarperCollins (1994)

Buss, D. M. and Kenrich, D. T., 'Evolutionary social psychology', in *The Handbook of Social Psychology* (4th ed.) D. T. Gilberts, S. T. Fiske and G. Lindzey (eds), Vol. 2, 982–1026, McGraw-Hill (1998)

Cabot, Dr Sandra, *Don't Let Your Hormones Rule Your Life*, Women's Health Advisory Service, Sydney (1991)

Calero, H., *Winning the Negotiation*, Hawthorn Books, New York (1979)

Camras, L. A., Oster, H., Campos, J. J., Miyake, K. and Bradshaw, D., 'Japanese and American infants, response to arm restraint', *Development Psychology*, 28, 578–83 (1992)

Cappella, J. N., 'The facial feedback hypothesis in human interaction: review and speculation', *Journal of Language and Social Psychology*, 12 (1993)

Carnegie, D., *How to Win Friends and Influence People*, Angus and Robertson, Sydney (1965)

Caro, M., *Caro's Book of Poker Tells*, Cardoza Publishing (2003)

Caro, *The Body Language of Poker*, Carol Publishing (1994)

Carper, Jean, *Your Miracle Brain*, HarperCollins (2000)

Casey, M. B., Brabeck, M. M. and Nuttall, R. L., 'As the twig is bent: the biology and socialisation of gender roles in women', *Brain and Cognition*, 27, 237–46 (1995)

Cashdan, E., 'Smiles, speech and body posture: how women and men display sociometric status and power', *Journal of Nonverbal Behavior*, 22 (4) (1998)

Cassidy, C. M., 'The good body: when big is better', *Medical Anthropology* (1991)

Castellow, W. A., Wuensch, K. L. and Moore, C. H., 'Effects of physical attractiveness of the plaintiff and defendant in sexual harassment judgements', *Journal of Social Behavior and Personality*, 5, 547–62 (1990)

Chang, K. T. and Antes, J. R., 'Sex and cultural differences in map reading', *The American Cartographer*, 14, 29–42 (1987)

Chaplin, W. F., Phillips, J. B., Brown, J. D. and Clanton, N. R., 'Handshaking, gender, personality, and first impressions', *Journal of Personality and Social Psychology*, 79 (1)

Chapman, A. J., 'Humor and laughter in social interaction and some implications for humor research' in P. McGhee and J. H. Goldstein (eds), *Handbook of Humor Research*, Vol. 1, basic issues, 135–57, Springer-Verlag (1983)

Clayton, P., *Body Language at Work*, Hamlyn (2003)

Coates, Jennifer, *Women, Men and Language* (2nd ed.), Longman (1993)

Cole, Julia, *After the Affair*, Vermilion (2000)

Collett, P., *The Book of Tells*, Doubleday (2003)

Collett, *Social Rules and Social Behaviour*, Blackwell, Oxford (1977)

Collis, Jack, *Yes You Can*, HarperCollins (1993)

Colton, H., *The Gift of Touch*, Seaview/Putnam (1996)

Cook, M., 'Experiments on orientation and proxemics', *Human Relations* (1970)

Cooper, K., *Bodybusiness*, AMA Com (1979)

Cox, Tracey, *Hot Relationships*, Bantam, Australia (1999)

Creagan, M., *Surfing Your Horizons*, Angus and Robertson (1996)

Crick, F. and Koch, C., 'Are we aware of neural activity in primary visual cortex?', *Nature* 375, 121–3 (1995)

Crick, *The Astonishing Hypothesis*, Macmillan, New York (1994)

Critchley, M., *Silent Language*, Butterworth, London (1975)

Critchley, *The Language of Gesture*, Arnold, London (1939)

Cundiff, M., *Kinesics*, Parker Publishing, New York (1972)

Dabbs, J. M., 'Testosterone, aggression and delinquency', *Second International Androgen Workshop*, 18–20 (February 1995)

Dabbs et al., 'Testosterone, crime and misbehaviour among 692 male prison inmates', *Pergamon*, Vol. 18 (5), 627–33 (1995)

Dabbs, 'Testosterone, smiling and facial appearance', *Journal of Non-verbal Behavior*, 21 (1992)

Dabbs, 'Age and seasonal variation in serum testosterone concentration among men', *Chronobiology International*, Vol. 7 (3), 245–9 (1990)

Dale-Guthrie, R., *Body Hot-Spots*, Van Nostrand Reinhold, New York (1976)

Dalgleish, T. and Power, M., *Handbook of Cognition and Emotion*, John Wiley & Sons (1999)

Damasio, Antonio R., *Descartes' Error: Emotion, Reason, and the Human Brain*, Avon Books (1995)

Danesi, M., *Of Cigarettes, High Heels, and Other Interesting Things*, Macmillan (1999)

Darwin, Charles, *The Voyage of the Beagle*, Doubleday, New York (1962)

Darwin, *The Expression of the Emotions in Man and Animals*, Philosophical Library (1872) with Introduction, Afterword and Commentary by Paul Ekman, HarperCollins; New York, Oxford University Press (1998)

Darwin, *The Descent of Man*, Murray, London, 569 (1871)

Davies, P., *Your Total Image*, Piatkus (1990)

Davis, K., 'Clinton and the truth: on the nose', *USA Today* (19 May 1999)

Davitz, J. R., *The Communication of Emotional Meaning*, McGraw-Hill, New York (1964)

Dawkins, R., *River Out of Eden: A Darwinian View of Life*, Basic Books, New York (1995)

Dawkins, *The Selfish Gene* (2nd ed.), Oxford University Press, New York (1990)

Dawkins, *The Blind Watchmaker*, Norton, New York (1987)

Dawkins, 'Universal Darwinism', in Bendall, D. S. (ed.), *Evolution from Molecules to Man*, Cambridge University Press, New York (1983)

De Angelis, Barbara, *Secrets about MEN Every Woman Should Know*, Dell, New York (1991)

De Lacoste, M. C., Holloway, R. L. and Woodward, D. J., 'Sex differences in the fetal corpus callosum', *Human Neurobiology*, 5, 93–6 (1986)

De Lacoste-Utamsing, C. and Hollaway, R. L., 'Sexual dimorphism in the human corpus callosum', *Science*, 216, 1431–2 (1982)

Deacon, Terrence, *The Symbolic Species: The Co-Evolution of Language and the Brain*, Norton, New York (1997)

Dedopulos, Tim, *The Ultimate Jokes Book*, Parragon Book Service (1998)

DeJong, F. H. and Van De Poll, N. E., *Relationship Between Sexual Behaviour in Male and Female Rats: Effects of Gonadal Hormones*, Elsevier, New York (1984)

Denenberg, V. H., Fitch, R. H., Schrott, L. M., Cowell, P. E. and Waters, N. S., 'Corpus callosum: interactive effects of infantile handling and testosterone in the rat', *Behavioural Neuroscience*, 105, 562–6 (1991)

DeVries, G. J., DeBruin, J. P. C., Uylings, H. B. M. and Corner, M. A. (eds.), *Differences in the Brain, Relationship Between Structure and Function*, Elsevier, New York (1984)

Diamond, Jared., *The Third Chimpanzee*, HarperCollins, New York (1992)

Dimberg, U., Thunberg, M. and Elmehed, K., 'Unconscious facial reactions to emotional facial expressions', *Psychological Science*, 11 (2000)

Dimberg and Ohman, A., 'Behold the wrath: psychophysiological responses to facial stimuli', *Motivation and Emotion*, 20, 149–82 (1996)

Dixon, N., *Our Own Worst Enemy*, Futura (1988)

Doran, G. D., 'Shake on it', *Entrepreneur Magazine* (July 1998)

Downs, A. C. and Lyons, P. M., 'Natural observations of the links between attractiveness and initial legal judgements', *Personality and Social Psychology Bulletin*, 17, 541–7 (1990)

Dubovsky, Steven L., *Mind–Body Deceptions*, Norton, New York (1997)

Duchenne de Boulogne, 'Recherches faites à l'aide du galvanisme sur l'état de la contractilité et de la sensibilité électro-musculaires dans les paralysies des membres supérieures', *Comptes rendus de l'Académie des sciences*, 29, 667–70 (1849)

Duncan, S. and Fiske, D. W., *Face-to-Face Interaction*, Erlbaum, Hillsdale, New Jersey (1977)

Dunkell, S., *Sleep Positions*, Heinemann, London (1977)

Eagly, A.H., Ashmore, R. D., Makhijani, M. G. and Longo L. C., 'What is beautiful is good but…: a meta-analytic review of research on the physical attractiveness stereotype', *Psychological Bulletin*, 110, 109–28 (1991)

Edelson, Edward, *Francis Crick and James Watson and the Building Blocks of Life*, Oxford University Press, New York (1998)

Edwards, Betty, *The New Drawing on the Right Side of the Brain*, J. P. Tarcher (1999)

Effron, D., *Gesture, Race and Culture*, Mouton, The Hague (1972)

Ehrhardt, A. A. and Meyer-Bahlburg, H. F. L., 'Effects of prenatal sex hormones on gender-related behaviour', *Science*, 211, 1312–14 (1981)

Eibl-Eibesfeldt, I., *Ethology: The Biology of Behavior* (2nd ed.), Holt, Rinehart & Winston, New York (1975)

Eibl-Eibesfeldt, *Love and Hate: The Natural History of Behaviour Patterns*, Holt, Rinehart & Winston (1971)

Ekman, Paul, *Telling Lies*, W. W. Norton (2002)

Ekman, 'Expression or communication about emotion', in N. Segal, G. E. Weisfeld and C. C. Weisfeld (eds), *Genetic, Ethological and Evolutionary Perspectives on Human Development: Essays in Honor of Dr Daniel G. Freedman*, American Psychiatric Association, Washington, DC (1997)

Ekman, 'Strong evidence for universals in facial expressions: a reply to Russell's mistaken critique', *Psychological Bulletin*, 115, 268–87 (1994)

Ekman and Davidson, R. J., 'Voluntary smiling changes regional brain activity', *Psychological Science*, 4, 342–5 (1993)

Ekman, 'Facial expression of emotion: new findings, new questions', *Psychological Science*, 3, 34–8 (1992)

Ekman, Davidson. R. J. and Friesen, W. V., 'The Duchenne smile: emotional expression and brain physiology II', *Journal of Personality and Social Psychology*, 58, 342–53 (1990)

Ekman and Heider, K. O., 'The universality of contempt expression: a replication', *Motivation and Emotion*,12, 303–8 (1988)

Ekman. P., Friesen, W. V., O'Sullivan, M., Chan, A., Diacoyanni-Tarlatzis. I., Heider, K., Krause, R., LeCompte, W. A., Pitcairn, T., Ricci-Bitti, P. E., Scherer, K. R., Tomita, M. and Tzavaras, A., 'Universals and cultural differences in the judgments of facial expressions of emotion', *Journal of Personality and Social Psychology*, 53, 712–17 (1987)

Ekman and Friesen, 'A new pan-cultural expression of emotion', *Motivation and Emotion*, 10, 159–68 (1986)

Ekman, Levenson, R. W. and Friesen, 'Autonomic nervous system activity distinguishes between emotions', *Science*, 221, 1208–10 (1983)

Ekman, 'About brows: emotional and conversational signals', in M. von Cranach, K. Foppa, W. Lepenies and D. Ploog, *Human Ethology*, Cambridge University Press, 169–248 (1979)

Ekman, 'Biological and cultural contributions to body and facial movement', in J. Blacking (ed.), *Anthropology of the Body*, Academic Press, 34–84, London (1977)

Ekman and Friesen, *Pictures of Facial Affect*, Consulting Psychologists Press (1976)

Ekman and Friesen, *Unmasking the Face*, Prentice-Hall, London (1975)

Ekman, 'Cross-cultural studies of facial expression' in P. Ekman (ed.), *Darwin and Facial Expression: A Century of Research in Review*, Academic Press, 169–222 (1973)

Ekman, 'Universals and cultural differences in facial expressions of emotion', in J. Cole (ed.), *Nebraska Symposium on Motivation*, University of Nebraska Press, 207–83 (1972)

Ekman, Friesen and Ellsworth, P., *Emotion in the Human Face*, Pergamon Press, New York (1972)

Ekman and Friesen, 'Constants across cultures in the face and emotion', *Journal of Personality and Social Psychology*, 17, 124–9 (1971)

Ekman, Friesen and Tomkins. S. S., 'Facial affect scoring technique: a first validity study', *Semiotica*, 3, 37–58 (1971)

Ekman and Friesen, 'The repertoire of nonverbal behavior: categories, origins, usage, and coding', *Semiotica*, 1, 49–98 (1969)

Ekman, Sorenson, E. R. and Friesen, 'Pan-cultural elements in facial displays of emotions', *Science*, 164 (3875), 86–8 (1969)

Elliot, A. J., *Child Language*, Cambridge University Press (1981)

Ellis, A. and Beattie, G., *The Psychology of Language and Communication*, Weidenfeld & Nicolson, London (1985)

Ellis, B. J. and Malamuth, N., 'Love and anger in romantic relationships: a discrete systems model', *Journal of Personality*, 68, 525–56 (2000)

Ellis, 'The evolution of sexual attraction: evaluative mechanisms in women', in J. H. Cosmides and J. Tooby, *The Adapted Mind: Evolutionary Psychology and the Generation of Culture*, Oxford University Press (1992)

Ellis, Havelock, *Man and Woman*, Ayer, North Stratford (1974)

Ellis, Lee, *Research Methods on the Social Sciences*, Minot State University (1994)

Ellyson, S. L. and Dovidio J. F., *Power, Dominance and Nonverbal Behaviour*, Springer-Verlag (1985)

Elsea, J. G., *First Impression Best Impression*, Simon & Schuster (1984)

Everhart, D. E. et al., 'Sex-related differences in event-related potentials, face recognition, and facial affect processing in prepubertal children', *Neuropsychology*, 15, 329–41 (July 2001)

Farah, Martha J., 'Is visual imagery really visual? Overlooked evidence from neuropsychology', *Psychological Review*, 95, 307–17 (1988)

Farrell, Dr Elizabeth and Westmore, Ann, *The HRT Handbook*, Anne O'Donovan, Australia (1993)

Farrell, Warren, *Women Can't Hear What Men Don't Say*, Finch Publishing, Australia (2001)

Fast, J. and B., *Reading Between the Lines*, Viking, New York (1979)

Fast, *Body Language*, Evans and Company/ Pan Books (1970)

Feldman, R. R. and Rime, B., *Fundamentals of Nonverbal Behaviour*, Cambridge University Press (1991)

Feldman, R. S., Forrest, J. A. and Happ, R. R., 'Self-presentation and verbal deception: do self-presenters lie more?', *Basic and Applied Social Psychology*, 24 (2) (2002)

Feldman, S., *Mannerisms of Speech and Gesture in Everyday Life*, International University Press (1959)

Ferris, Stewart, *How to Chat-Up Women*, Summersdale Publishers (1994)

Fisher, Helen, *The First Sex*, Random House, London (1999)

Fisher, *Anatomy of Love: The Natural History of Monogamy, Adultery, and Divorce*, Norton, New York (1992)

Foot, H. C. and Chapman, A. J., 'The social responsiveness of young children in humorous situations', in A. J. Chapman and H. C. Foot (eds), *Humour and Laughter: Theory, Research, and Applications*, 187–214, Wiley, London (1976)

French, Scott and Van Houten, Paul, PhD, *Never Say Lie: How to Beat the Machines, the Interviews, the Chemical Tests*, Palladin Press, Boulder, Colorado (1987)

Freud, Sigmund, *Three Contributions to the Theory of Sex*, Random House, New York (1905)

Fromm, Erich, *The Forgotten Language*, Grove Press, Inc., New York (1951)

Furnham, A., Dias, M. and McClelland, A., 'The role of body weight, waist-to-hip ratio, and breast size in judgements of female attractiveness', *Sex Roles*, 3/4 (1998)

Gardner, Howard, *Extraordinary Minds*, Basic Books, New York (1998)

Garner, Alan, *Conversationally Speaking* (2nd ed.), Lowell House, Los Angeles (1997)

Gayle, W., *Power Selling*, Prentice-Hall, New York (1959)

Gazzaniga, Michael S. (ed.) *The New Cognitive Neurosciences*, MIT Press (1999)

Ghiglieri, Michael P., *The Dark Side of Man*, Perseus Books (1999)

Gilmartin, P. P., 'Maps, mental imagery, and gender in the recall of geographical information', *The American Cartographer* 13, 335–44 (1986)

Gilmartin and Patton, J. C., 'Comparing the sexes on spatial abilities; map-use skills', *Annals of the Association of American Geographer*, 74, 605–19 (1984)

Glass, L., *I Know What You're Thinking: Using the Four Codes of Reading People to Improve Your Life*, John Wiley & Sons, Inc. (2002)

Glass, *He Says, She Says*, Putnam, New York (1992)

Gochros, Harvey, and Fischer, Joel, *Treat Yourself to a Better Sex Life*, Englewood Cliffs, Prentice-Hall, New Jersey (1986)

Goffman, Erving, *Gender Advertisements*, Harper, New York (1976)

Goffman, *Interaction Ritual*, Allen Lane, London (1972)

Goffman, *Behaviour in Public Places*, Free Press, Illinois (1963)

Goffman, *The Presentation of Self in Everyday Life*, Edinburgh University Press (1956)

Goleman, Daniel, *Emotional Intelligence: Why It Can Matter More Than IQ*, Bantam, New York (1997)

Goodall, J., *The Chimpanzees of Gombe*, Harvard University Press (1986)

Goodheart, A., *Laughter Therapy: How to Laugh About Everything In Your Life That Isn't Really Funny*

Gordon, R. L., *Interviewing Strategy, Techniques and Tactics*, Dorsey, Homewood, Illinois (1976)

Gorski, R. A., 'Sex differences in the rodent brain: their nature and origin', in Reinsch, J. M. et al. (eds.), *Masculinity and Femininity*, Oxford University Press, 37–67 (1987)

Gottman, J. M., Murray, J. D., Swanson, C. C., Tyson, R. and Swanson,

K. R., *The Mathematics of Marriage: Dynamic Nonlinear Models*, MIT Press (Bradford Books), Cambridge, Massachusetts (2003)

Gottman and Silver, N., *The Seven Principles for Making Marriage Work*, Crown Publishers (1999)

Grammer, K., Kruck, K. B. and Magnusson, M. S., 'The courtship dance: patterns of nonverbal synchronization in opposite-sex encounters', *Journal of Nonverbal Behavior*, 22, 3–29 (1998)

Grammer, 'Strangers meet: laughter and nonverbal signs of interest in opposite-sex encounters', *Journal of Nonverbal Behavior*, 14, 209–36 (1990)

Gray, John, *Mars and Venus in the Bedroom*, HarperCollins, New York (1995)

Gray, *Men, Women and Relationships*, Hodder & Stoughton, Australia (1995)

Gray, *What Your Mother Couldn't Tell You and Your Father Didn't Know*, HarperCollins, New York (1994)

Gray, *Men Are From Mars, Women Are From Venus*, HarperCollins, New York (1993)

Gray, *Men, Women & Relationships* (2nd ed.), Hillsboro, OR: Beyond Words (1993)

Greenfield, Susan, *Journey to the Centers of the Mind*, Basic Books, New York (1998)

Greenfield, *The Human Brain: A Guided Tour*, Basic Books (1997)

Greenfield, *The Human Mind Explained: An Owner's Guide to the Mysteries of the Mind*, Henry Holt, New York (1996)

Grice, Julia, *What Makes a Woman Sexy*, Dodd, Mead, New York (1998)

Griffin, J., *How to Say It at Work: Putting Yourself Across with Power Words, Phrases, Convincing Body Language, and Communication Secrets*, NYIF (1998)

Gron, G. et al., 'Brain activation during human navigation: gender-different neural networks as substrate of performance', *Nature Neuroscience*, 3, 404–8 (2000)

Grotius, Hugo, *On the Law of War and Peace*, translated by F. Kelsey, Bobbs-Merrill, Indianapolis (1925) [Defines lying in terms of the rights of those to whom the lie is addressed.]

Gschwandtner, G., with Garnett, P., *Non-Verbal Selling Power*, Prentice-Hall (1985)

Gur, R. and Gur, R., 'Sex and handedness differences in cerebral blood flow, during rest and cognitive activity', *Science*, 217, 659–61 (1982)

Gur, R. C. et al., 'An FMRI study of sex differences in regional activation to a verbal and a spatial task', *Brain and Language*, 74, 157–70 (2000)

Gur et al., 'Sex differences in brain gray and white matter in healthy young adults: correlations with cognitive performance', *Journal of Neuroscience* 19, 4065–72 (1999)

Haig, D., 'Genetic imprinting and the theory of parent-offspring conflict', *Developmental Biology*, 3, 153–60 (1992)

Hall, E. T., *The Hidden Dimension*, Doubleday, New York (1966)

Hall, *Silent Language*, Doubleday, New York (1959)

Hammersmith, D. and Biddle, J. E., 'Beauty and the Labor Market', *American Economic Review*, 84, 1174–94 (1994)

Hampson, E. and Kimura, D., 'Sex differences and hormonal influences on cognitive function in humans', in Becker, J. B., Breedlove, S. M. and Crews, D. (ed.), *Behavioural Endocrinology*, MIT Press, Cambridge, Massachusetts, 357–400 (1992)

Hampson and Kimura, 'Reciprocal effects of hormonal fluctuations on human motor and perceptospatial skills', *Research Bulletin*, 656, Department of Psychology, University of Western Ontario, London, Ontario, Canada (June 1987)

Handy, Charles, *The Empty Raincoat: Making Sense of the Future*, Hutchinson, London (1994)

Harlow, H. F. and Zimmerman, R. R., 'The development of affectional responses in infant monkeys', *Journal of the American Philosophical Society*, 102, 501–9 (1958)

Harpending, H., 'Gene frequencies, DNA sequences, and human origins', *Perspectives in Biology and Medicine*, 37, 384–95 (1994)

Harper, R. G., *Non-Verbal Communication: the State of the Art*, John Wiley, New York (1978)

Harrelson, Leonard, *Lie Test: Deception, Truth and the Polygraph*, Partners Publishing Group (1998)

Hatfield, E. and Rapson, R. L., *Love, Sex and Intimacy: Their Psychology, Biology, and History*, HarperCollins, New York (1993)

Hecht, M. A. and LaFrance, M., 'License or obligation to smile: the effect of power and gender on amount and type of smiling', *Personality and Social Psychology Bulletin*, 24, 1326–36 (1988)

Heisse, John W. Jr, MD, *The Verimetrics Computer System: A Reliability Study*, self-published, Burlington, Vermont (1992)

Heisse, *Audio Stress Analysis: A Validation and Reliability Study of the Psychological Stress Evaluator (PSE)*, self-published, Burlington, Vermont (1976)

Heisse, 'The 14 Question Modified Zone of Comparison Test', *Stressing Comments*, International Society of Stress Analysts, Vol. 3, No. 7, 1–4 (June 1975)

Heisse, *Simplified Chart Reading*, self-published, Burlington, Vermont (1974)

Hendrix, Harville, PhD, *Getting the Love You Want: A Guide for Couples*, HarperCollins, New York (1990)

Henley, N., 'Body politics', in A. Branaman, *Self and Society*, Blackwell (2001)

Henley, N. *Body Politics: Power, Sex and Non-Verbal Communication*, Prentice-Hall (1977)

Hess, E., *The Tell-Tale Eye*, Van Nostrand Reinhold, New York (1975)

Heyes, C. M. and Galef, B. G., *Social Learning in Animals: The Roots of Culture*, Academic Press, New York (1996)

Hillary, E., *View from the Summit*, Doubleday (1999)

Hind, R., *Non-Verbal Communication*, Cambridge University Press (1972)

Hite, Shere, *Women and Love*, Knopf, New York (1987)

Hobson, J. Allan, *Consciousness*, W. H. Freeman, New York (1998)

Hobson, *The Chemistry of Conscious States: How the Brain Changes Its Mind*, Little, Brown, Boston (1994)

Hodgson, D. H., *Consequences of Utilitarianism*, Oxford (1967)

Holden, Robert, *Shift Happens*, Hodder & Stoughton (1998)

Holden, *Laughter the Best Medicine*, Thorsons (1993)

Hopkins, W. D., Bales, S. A. and Bennett, A. J., 'Heritability of hand preferences in chimpanzees', *International Journal of Neuroscience*, 74 (1994)

Hore, T., *Non-Verbal Behaviour*, Australian Council for Educational Research (1976)

Horvath, Frank, PhD, 'Detecting deception: the promise and the reality of voice stress analysis', *Journal of Forensic Sciences*, Vol. 27, No. 2, 340–51 (1982)

Hoyenga K. B. and Hoyenga, K. T., *Gender-Related Differences*, Allyn & Bacon, 343–5 (1993)

Hoyenga, op cit., 321–2; Mann, V. et al., 'Sex differences in cognitive abilities: a cross-cultural perspective', *Neuropsychologia*, Vol. 28, 1063–77 (1990)

Hoyenga, Blick, and Kermit T. Hoyenga, *The Question of Sex Differences*, Little, Brown, Boston (1979)

Hu, S. et al., 'Linkage between sexual orientation and chromosome Xq28 in males but not females', *Nature Genetics* 11, 248–56 (1995)

Humphrey, Nicholas, *A History of the Mind*, Simon & Schuster, New York (1992)

Humphrey, 'Contrast Illusions in Perspective', *Nature*, 232, 91–93 (1970)

Hutchinson, John B. (ed.), *Biological Determinants of Sexual Behaviour*, John Wiley, New York (1978)

Huxley, Aldous, *The Doors of Perception*, Harper, New York (1963)

Inbau, Fred E. and Reid, John E., *Truth and Deception: The Polygraph ('Lie Detector') Technique*, Williams & Wilking Co., Baltimore (1969)

James, W., *Principles of Psychology*, Holt, Rinehart, New York (1892)

Jensen, Eric, *Brain-Based Learning*, Brain Store, Inc. (2000)

Johnson, Gary, *Monkey Business*, Gower Publishing (1995)

Juan, Dr Stephen, *The Odd Body and Brain*, HarperCollins, Australia (2001)

Jung, C., *Man and His Symbols*, Aldus, London (1964)

Kagan, J., 'Sex differences in the human infant', in McGill, Thomas E. et al. (ed.), *Sex and Behaviour: Status and Prospectus*, Plenum, New York (1978)

Kahn, Elayne J., and Rudnitsky, David A., *Love Codes: How to Decipher Men's Secret Signals About Romance*, NAL-Dutton, New York (1992)

Kahn and Rudnitsky, *Love Codes*, Piatkus (1989)

Kahn and Cannell, C. F., *The Dynamics of Interviewing*, Wiley, New York (1957)

Kant, Immanuel, 'On a supposed right to lie from benevolent motives', in *The Critique of Practical Reason and Other Writings in Moral Philosophy*, University of Chicago Press (1949)

Keating, C. F., 'Human dominance signals: the primate in us', in S. L. Ellyson and J. F. Dovidio, *Power, Dominance, and Non-Verbal Behaviour*, Springer-Verlag (1985)

Keating and Keating, E. G., 'Visual scan patterns of rhesus monkeys viewing faces', *Perception*, 11, 211–19 (1982)

Kendon, A., 'Some relationships between body motion and speech: an analysis of an example', in A. W. Siegman and B. Pope (eds), *Studies in Dyadic Communication*, Pergamon Press (1994)

Kendon, *Organisation of Behaviour in Face-to-Face Interaction*, Mouton, The Hague (1975)

Kenton, Leslie, *Ten Steps to a Young YOU*, Vermilion (1996)

Key, M. R., *Non-Verbal Communication: A Research Guide and Bibliography*, Scarecrow Press, Metuchen, New Jersey (1977)

Kimura, D., 'Sex, sexual orientation and sex hormones influence human cognitive function', *Current Opinion in Neurobiology*, 6, 259–63 (1996)

Kimura, 'Estrogen replacement therapy may protect against intellectual decline in post-menopausal women', *Hormones and Behaviour*, 29, 312–321 (1995)

Kimura and Hampson E., 'Cognitive pattern in men and women is influenced by fluctuations in sex hormones', *Current Directions in Psychological Science* 3, 57–61 (1994)

Kimura, *Neuromotor Mechanisms in Human Communication*, Oxford University Press, New York (1993)

Kimura, 'Sex differences in the brain', *Scientific American*, 267, 118–25 (1992)

Kimura, 'Are men's and women's brains really different?', *Canadian Psycol.*, 28 (2), 133–47 (1987)

Kimura, 'How Different are the male and female brains?', *Orbit*, 17, No. 3, 13–14 (October 1986)

Kimura, 'Male brain, female brain: the hidden difference', *Psychology Today*, 51–8 (November 1985)

Kimura and Harshman, R., 'Sex differences in brain organisation for verbal and non-verbal function', *Progress in Brain Research*, 61, De Vreis, G. J. et al. (eds.), Elsevier, Amsterdam, 423–40 (1984)

King, Dr Rosie, *Good Loving, Great Sex*, Random House, Australia (1997)

King, N., *The First Five Minutes*, Simon & Schuster (1988)

Kinsey A. C., Pomeroy W. B. and Martin C. E., *Sexual Behaviour in the Human Male*, Saunders, Philadelphia (1948)

Knapp, M., *Non-Verbal Communication in Human Interaction* (2nd ed.), Holt, Rinehart & Winston, New York (1978)

Knight, S., *NLP at Work: The Difference that Makes a Difference in Business*, Nicholas Brealey Publishing (2002)

Korda, M., *Power in the Office*, Weidenfeld & Nicolson, London (1976)

Korda, *Power! How To Get It, How To Use It*, Weidenfeld & Nicolson, London (1975)

Korman, B., *Hands: The Power of Awareness*, Sunridge Press, New York (1978)

Kreeger, K. Y., 'Yes, Biologically Speaking, Sex Does Matter', *The Scientist*, 16 (1), 35–6 (7 January 2002)

Kriete, R. and Stanley, R., 'A Comparison of the Psychological Stress Evaluator and the Polygraph', presented at the First Annual Seminar of the International Society of Stress Analysts, Chicago (1974)

Kulka, R. A. and Kessler, J. R., 'Is justice really blind? The effect of litigant physical attractiveness on judicial judgement', *Journal of Applied Social Psychology*, 4, 336–81 (1978)

Kumler and Butterfield, *Gender Difference in Map Reading*, University of Colorado (1998)

LaFrance, M. and Hecht, M. A., 'Why do women smile more than men?', in A. Fischer (ed.), *Gender and Emotions*, 118–42, Cambridge University Press (2000)

LaFrance and Hecht, 'A meta-analysis of sex differences in smiling', in A. Fischer (ed.), *Non-Verbal Communication and Gender*, Cambridge University Press (1999)

LaFrance and Hecht, 'Option or obligation to smile: the effect of power and gender on facial expression', in P. Philippot, R. S. Feldman and E. J. Coats (eds), *The Social Context of Non-Verbal Behaviour*, Cambridge University Press (1999)

LaFrance and Hecht, 'Why smiles generate leniency', *Personality and Social Psychology Bulletin*, 21, 207–14 (1995)

Lakoff, Robin, *Language and Woman's Place*, Harper, New York (1976)

Lamb, W., *Body Code*, Routledge and Kegan Paul, London (1979)

Lamb, *Posture and Gesture*, Duckworth, London (1965)

Lambert, D., *Body Language*, HarperCollins (1996)

LeVay, S. *The Sexual Brain*, MIT Press, Cambridge, Massachusetts (1993)

Lewis, C. et al., 'The prevalence of specific arithmetic difficulties and specific reading difficulties in 9- to 10-year-old boys and girls', *Journal of Child Psychological Psychiatry*, Vol. 35 (2), 283–92 (1994)

Lewis, D., *The Secret Language of Success*, Carroll & Graf (1990)

Lewis, *The Secret Language of Your Child*, Souvenir Press, London (1978)

Lewis, *Convention: A Philosophical Study*, Harvard University Press, Cambridge, Massachusetts (1969)

Lewis, M. and Sarrni, C., *Lying and Deception in Everyday Life*, Guilford Press (1993)

Lewis and Cherry, Linda, 'Social behaviour and language acquisition', in Lewis, Michael and Leonard A. (ed.), *Rosenblum Interaction, Conversation, and the Development of Language*, John Wiley, New York (1977)

Lewis, 'Culture and gender roles: there is no unisex in the nursery', *Psychology Today*, 5, 54–7 (1972)

Lieberman, David J., *Never Be Lied to Again*, St Martin's Press (2000)

Liggett, J., *The Human Face*, Constable, London (1974)

Lippold, O., 'Physiological Tremor', *Scientific American*, Vol. 224, No. 3, 65–73 (1971)

Lloyd, B. and Archer, J., *Sex and Gender*, Penguin Books, London (1982)

Lloyd-Elliott, M., *Secrets of Sexual Body Language*, Hamlyn (1995)

Logie, R. H., *Visuospatial Working Memory*, Hillsdale, New Jersey, Erlbaum (1995)

Lorenz, Konrad, *On Aggression*, Harcourt, New York (1974)

Lorenz, *King Solomon's Ring*, London Reprint Society (1953)

Lowndes, L., *How to Talk to Anyone: 101 Little Communication Tricks for Big Success in Relationships*, Contemporary Books (2003)

Lyle, J., *Understanding Body Language*, Hamlyn (1989)

Maccoby, Eleanor and Jacklin, Carol N., *The Psychology of Sex Differences*, Stanford University Press (1974)

MacHovec, F. J., *Body Talk*, Peter Pauper Press, New York (1975)

Mack, C. M., Boehm, G. W., Berrebi, A. S. and Denenberg, V. H., 'Sex differences in the distribution of axon types within the genu of the rat corpus callosum', *Brain Research*, 697, 152–6 (1995)

Malandro, L. A. and Barker, L., *Nonverbal Communication*, Addison-Wesley (1983)

Mallery, G., *The Gesture Speech of Man*, Salem (1881)

Marcel, A. J., 'Conscious and preconscious perception: experiments on visual masking and word recognition', *Cognitive Psychology*, 15, 197–237 (1983)

Marr, D. and Nishihara, H. K., 'Representation and recognition of the spatial organization of three-dimensional shapes', *Proceedings of the Royal Society of London*, B, 200, 269–94 (1978)

Marshall, Hillie, *The Good Dating Guide*, Summersdale Publishers (1998)

Martin P., *The Sickening Mind*, HarperCollins (1998)

Masters, W. H. and Johnson, V. E., *Human Sexual Response*, Little, Brown, Boston (1966)

Maynard, Smith J., *The Theory of Evolution*, Cambridge University, New York (1993)

Maynard-Smith, *Did Darwin Get It Right?*, Penguin, New York (1993)

McCormack, S. A. and Parks, M. R., 'What women know that men don't: sex differences in determining the truth behind deceptive messages', *Journal of Social and Personal Relationships*, 7 (1990)

McCroskey, Larson and Knapp, *An Introduction to Interpersonal Behaviour*, Prentice-Hall, Englewood Cliffs, New Jersey (1971)

McGee, M. G., *Human Spatial Abilities: Sources of Sex Differences*, Praeger Press, New York (1979)

McGuiness, D., 'How schools discriminate against boys', *Human Nature*, 82–8 (February 1979)

McIntosh, D. N., 'Facial feedback hypothesis: evidence, implications, and directions', *Motivation and Emotion*, 20 (1996)

McKinlay, Deborah, *Love Lies*, HarperCollins, London (1994)

Mehrabian, A., *Silent Messages*, Wadsworth, Belmont, California (1971)

Mehrabian, *Tactics in Social Influence*, Prentice-Hall, Englewood Cliffs, New Jersey (1969)

Millar, M. G. and Millar, K., 'Detection of deception in familiar and unfamiliar persons: the effects of information restriction', *Journal of Nonverbal Behavior*, 19 (2) (1995)

Millard, Anne, *Early Man*, Pan, London (1981)

Miller, A., 'Re-dressing classical statuary: the eighteenth-century "Hand-in-Waistcoat" portrait', *Art Bulletin* (College Art Association of America), Vol. 77, No. 2, 45–64 (March 1995)

Miller, Geoffrey F., *The Mating Mind: How Sexual Choice Shaped the Evolution of Human Nature*, Doubleday, London (2000)

Miller, Gerald R. and Stiff, James B., *Deception Communication*, Sage Publications, Newbury Park (1993)

Miller, S. K., 'Gene hunters sound warning over gay link', *New Scientist*, 4–5 (24 July 1993)

Mitchell, M. E., *How to Read the Language of the Face*, Macmillan, New York (1968)

Moir, Anne and Bill, *Why Men Don't Iron*, HarperCollins Publishers (1998)

Moir and Jessel, David, *BrainSex*, Dell, New York (1992)

Money, J., 'Ablatio penis: normal male infant sex-reassignment as a girl', *Archives of Sexual Behaviour*, 4, 65–71 (1975)

Money and Erhdardt, A. A., *Man and Woman, Boy and Girl: The Differentiation and Dimorphism of Gender Identity from Conception to Maturity*, Johns Hopkins University Press, Baltimore, Maryland (1972)

Money and Erhdart, 'Progestin-induced hermaphroditism: IQ and psycho-sexual identity in the study of ten girls', *Journal of Sex Research*, 3, 83–100 (1967)

Montagu, A., *Touching: The Human Significance of the Skin*, Columbia University Press (1971)

Moore, C. L., 'Maternal behaviour of rats is affected by hormonal condition of pups', *Journal of Comparative and Physiological Psychology*, 1, 123–9 (1982)

Morris, Desmond, *People Watching*, Vintage (2002)

Morris, *Bodytalk*, Jonathan Cape (1994)

Morris, *Babywatching*, Jonathan Cape (1991)

Morris, *Animalwatching*, Crown, New York (1990)

Morris and Marsh, P., *Tribes*, Pyramid (1988)

Morris with Collett, Marsh and O'Shaughnessy, *Gestures, Their Origins and Distribution*, Cape, London (1979)

Morris, *Manwatching*, Jonathan Cape/Abrahams (1977)

Morris, *Initmate Behaviour*, Cape/Random House (1971)

Morris, *The Human Zoo*, Cape (1969)

Morris, *The Naked Ape*, Cape/Dell (1967)

Moyer, K. E., 'Sex differences in aggression', in Friedman et al. (ed.), *Sex Differences in Behaviour*, John Wiley, New York (1974)

Nierenberg, G. and Calero, H., *How to Read a Person like a Book*, Hawthorn Books, New York (1971)

Nierenberg, *The Art of Negotiating*, Hawthorn Books (1968)

O'Connell, S., *Mindreading: An Investigation Into How We Learn to Love and Lie*, Doubleday (1998)

O'Connor, Dagmar, *How to Make Love to the Same Person for the Rest of Your Life and Still Love It*, Bantam, New York (1986)

O'Connor, J., *NLP: A Practical Guide to Achieving the Results You Want*, HarperCollins (2001)

O'Connor and Seymour, J., *Introducing NLP Neuro-Linguistic Programming*, HarperCollins (1993)

O'Neill, W. C., 'Report of the Special Hearing Officer of the Secretary of State of Florida, Regarding Public Hearings of the Department of State of Florida: Psychological Stress Evaluation', Florida Secretary of State, Tallahassee, Florida (1974)

O'Toole, George, *The Assassination Tapes: An Electronic Probe into the Murder of John F. Kennedy and the Dallas Cover-Up*, Penthouse Press, New York (1975)

Ornstein, Robert E., *The Right Mind: Making Sense of the Hemispheres*, Harcourt, New York (1997)

Pattatucci, A. M. L. and Hamer, D. H., 'Development and familiarity of sexual orientation in females', *Behaviour Genetics*, 25, 407–20 (1995)

Patterson, J., *The Day America Told the Truth*, Plume (1992)

Pease, A., *Rude and Politically Incorrect Jokes*, Pease Training International (1998)

Pease, with Garner, Alan, *Talk Language*, Simon & Schuster (1998)

Pease, A., *Everything Men Know About Women*, Camel Publishing, Sydney (1986)

Pease, Allan, *Signals: How to Use Body Language for Power, Success and Love*, Bantam Books, New York (1984)

Pease, Allan and Barbara, *The Definitive Book of Body Language*, Orion (2006)

Pease, A. and B., *Why Men Don't Have a Clue & Women Always Need More Shoes*, Orion (2006)

Pease, A. and B., *Why Men Can Only Do One Thing at a Time & Women Won't Stop Talking*, Orion (2003)

Pease, A. and B., *Why Men Don't Listen & Women Can't Read Maps*, Orion (2001)

Pease, A. and B., *Memory Language*, Pease Learning Systems, Sydney (1993)

Pease, A. V., *The Hot Button Selling System*, Elvic & Co., Sydney (1976)

Pease, R. V. and Dr Ruth, *My Secret Life As a Porn Star*, Camel Publishing, Sydney (2004)

Pease, R., and Dr Ruth, *My Secret life As a Gigolo*, Pease International (2002)

Pease, R., and Dr Ruth, *Tap Dance Your Way to Social Ridicule*, Pease Training International (1998)

Peck, M. Scott, *The Road Less Traveled*, Simon & Schuster, New York (1985)

Penny, Alexandra, *How to Keep Your Man Monogamous*, Bantam Books (1990)

Perper, T., *Sex Signals: The Biology of Love*, ISI Press (1985)

Pertot, Dr Sandra, *A Commonsense Guide to Sex*, HarperCollins, Sydney (1984)

Peters, Brooks, *Terrific Sex in Fearful Times*, St Martin's Press, New York (1988)

Petras, Kathryn and Petras, Ross, *The 776 Stupidest Things Ever Said*, Doubleday, New York (1993)

Pillard, R. C. and Bailey, J. M., *Archives of Sexual Behaviour*, 24, 1–20 (1195); 'Human sexual orientation has a heritable component', *Human Biology*, 70, 347–65 (1998)

Pillard and Bailey, 'A biologic perspective on sexual orientation', *The Psychiatric Clinics of North America*, 18, 71–84 (1995)

Pinker, S., *How the Mind Works*, W. W. Norton (1997)

Pittman, Frank, *Private Lies*, Norton (1990)

Place, U. T., 'The role of the hand in the evolution of language', *Psycoloquy*, 11 (2000)

Platt, Vanessa Lloyd, *Secrets of Relationship Success*, Vermilion (2000)

Pliner, O., Kramer, L. and Alloway, T., *Non-Verbal Communication*, Plenum Press, New York (1973)

Provine, R. R., *Laughter: A Scientific Investigation*, Penguin (2000)

Provine, *Yawns, Laughs, Smiles and Talking: Naturalistic and Laboratory Studies of Facial Action and Social Communication* (1997)

Provine, and Yong, Y. L., 'Laughter: a stereotyped human vocalization', *Ethology*, 89 (2), 115–24 (1991)

Provine and Fischer, K. R., 'Laughing, smiling and talking: relation to sleeping and social context in humans', *Ethology*, 83 (4), 295–305 (1989)

Provine, 'Contagious yawning and laughter: significance for sensory features, and the evolution of social behaviour'

Pujol, J., Deus, J., Losilla, J. M. and Capdevila, A., 'Cerebral lateralization of language in normal left-handed people studied by functional MRI', *Neurology*, 52 (1999)

Quilliam, Susan, *Sexual Body Talk*, Headline (1992)

Quilliam, *Body Language Secrets*, HarperCollins (1997)

Quilliam, *Your Child's Body Language*, Angus and Robertson (1994)

Rabin, Claire, *Equal Partners, Good Friends: Empowering Couples Through Therapy*, Routledge, London (1996)

Reid, John E., Inbau, Fred E. and Buckley, Joseph B., *Criminal Interrogation and Confessions*, Williams & Wilkins Co., Baltimore (1986)

Reik, T., *Listening with the Third Ear*, Farrar, Straus & Giroux, New York (1948)

Reinisch, J. M. et al. (eds.), *Masculinity–Femininity*, The Kinsey Institute Series, Oxford University Press (1987)

Reisner, Paul, *Couplehood*, Bantam, New York (1994)

Ridley, Matt, *The Red Queen: Sex and the Evolution of Human Nature*, Macmillan, New York (1993)

Ringer, R. J., *Winning Through Intimidation*, Fawcett Crest, Los Angeles (1973)

Robbins, Jim, *A Symphony in the Brain: The Evolution of the New Brain Wave Biofeedback*, Atlantic Monthly Press (2000)

Robinson, J., *Body Packaging*, Watermark Press (1988)

Roffman, Howard, *Presumed Guilty*, A. S. Barnes and Company, Inc., New York (1976)

Rogers, Lesley, *Sexing the Brain*, Weidenfeld & Nicolson (1999)

Rogers, 'Behavioural, structural and neurochemical asymmetries in the avian brain: a model system for studying visual development and processing', *Neuroscience and Biobehavioral Reviews*, 20, 487–503 (1996)

Roger, *The Development of Brain and Behaviour in the Chicken*, CAB International, Wallingford (1995)

Rosenblum, L. A., 'Sex differences in mother-infant attachment in monkeys', in Friedman, R. et al. (ed.) *Sex Differences in Behaviour*, John Wiley, New York (1974)

Russell, J. A. and Fernandez-Dols, J. M. (eds), *The Psychology of Facial Expression*, 158–75, Cambridge University Press (1997)

Russell, 'Facial expressions of emotion: what lies beyond minimal universality?', *Psychological Bulletin*, 118, 379–91 (1995)

Russell, 'Is there universal recognition of emotion from facial expression? A review of cross-cultural studies', *Psychological Bulletin*, 115, 102–41 (1994)

Russell, Suzuki, N. and Ishida, N., 'Canadian, Greek, and Japanese freely produced emotion labels for facial expression', *Motivation and Emotion*, 17, 337–51 (1993)

Russo, N., 'Connotation of seating arrangement', *Cornell Journal of Social Relations* (1967)

Saitz, R. L. and Cervenka, E. C., *Handbook of Gestures: Columbia and the United States*, Mouton, The Hague (1972)

Samenow, Stanton E., *Inside the Criminal Mind*, Times Books, New York (1984)

Sathre, F., Olson, R. and Whitney, C., *Let's Talk*, Scott Foresman, Glenview Illinois (1973)

Scheflen, A. E., *Body Language and the Social Order*, Prentice-Hall (1981)

Scheflen, 'On communicational processes', in A. Wolfgang (ed.), *Nonverbal Behavior: Applications and Cultural Implications*, 1–16, Academic Press (1979)

Scheflen, *Human Territories*, Prentice-Hall, New Jersey (1976)

Scheflen, *How Behavior Means*, Garden City, Anchor (1975)

Scheflen, 'Quasi-courtship behavior', in S. Weitz (ed.), *Nonverbal Communication*, 182–98, Oxford University Press (1974)

Schipp, Thomas, PhD and Kryzysztof, Izdebski, 'Current evidence for the existence of laryngeal macrotremor and microtremor', *Journal of Forensic Sciences* (1980)

Schultz, A. H., 'Proportions, variability and asymmetries of the fones of the limbs and the clavicles in man and apes', *Human Biology*, 9 (1937)

Schutz, W. C., *A Three-Dimensional Theory of Interpersonal Behaviour*, Holt, Rinehart & Winston, New York (1958)

Self, C. M., Gopal, S., Golledge, R. G. and Fenstermaker, S., 'Gender-related differences in spatial abilities', *Progress in Human Geography*, 16, 315–42 (1992)

Shapiro, R., *Origins*, Pelican, London (1988)

Shaywitz, B. A. et al., 'Sex differences in the functional organization of the brain for language', *Nature*, 373, 607–9 (1995)

Shaywitz, Sally and Bennett, 'How is the brain formed?', *Nature*, 373, 607–9 (1995)

Siddons, H., *Practical Illustration of Rhetorical Gestures*, London (1822)

Singh, D. and Young, R. K., 'Body weight, waist-to-hip ratio, breasts, and hips: role in judgements of female attractiveness and desirability for relationships', *Ethology and Sociobiology*, 16 (1995)

Sommer, R., *Personal Space: The Behavioural Basis of Design*, Prentice-Hall, Englewood Cliffs, New Jersey (1969)

Staheli, Lana, *Affair-Proof Your Marriage*, Staheli Inc. (1995)

Steel, J. and Mays, S., 'Handedness and directional asymmetry in the long bones of the human upper limb', *International Journal of Osteoarchaeology*, 5 (1995)

Steele, D., *Body Language Secrets: A Guide During Courtship and Dating*, SBP (1999)

Stein, D. G., 'Brain damage, sex hormones and recovery: a new role for progesterone and estrogen?', *Trends in Neuroscience*, 24, 386–91 (July 2001)

Stewart, J. E. II, 'Defendant's attractiveness as a factor in the outcome of trials', *Journal of Applied Social Psychology*, 10, 348–61 (1980)

Stickels, Terry, *Are You As Smart As You Think?: 150 Original Mathematical, Logical, and Spatial-Visual Puzzles for All Levels of Puzzle Solvers*, Griffin (2000)

Strack, F., Martin, L. and Stepper, S., 'Inhibiting and facial conditions of the human smile: a nonobtrusive test of the facial feedback hypothesis', *Journal of Personality and Social Psychology*, 54 (1988)

Strodtbeck, F. and Hook, L., 'The social dimensions of a twelve-man jury table', *Sociometry* (1961)

Stumpf, H. and Klieme, E., 'Sex-related differences in spatial ability: more evidence for convergence', *Perceptual and Motor Skills*, 69, Part 1, 915–21 (1989)

Suter, W. A., *My Life As a She-Man*, Camel Publishing (2004)

Suter, William and Beatrice, *Guilt Without Sex*, Pease Training International (1998)

Swaab, D. F. and Hofman, M. A., 'Sexual differentiation of the human hypothalamus in relation to gender and sexual orientation', *Trends in Neurosciences*, 18, 264–70 (1996)

Swaab, 'Development of the Human Hypothalamus', *Neurochem Research*, Vol. 20 (5), 509–19 (May 1995)

Swaab and Hofman, 'Sexual differentiation of the human brain', *Progress in Brain Research*, 61, De Vries, G. J. et al. (eds), Elsevier, Amsterdam (1984)

Szasz, S., *Body Language of Children*, Norton, New York (1978)

Tannen, Deborah, *Talking from 9 to 5*, Morrow, New York (1994)

Tannen, *You Just Don't Understand: Women and Men in Conversation*, New York: Morrow (1990)

Tannen, *That's Not What I Meant*, Ballantine, New York (1986)

Tarr, M. J. and Pinker, S., 'Mental rotation and orientation-dependence in shape recognition', *Cognitive Psychology*, 21, 233–82 (1989)

Tarr, 'Rotating objects to recognize them', *Psychonomic Bulletin and Review*, 2, 55–82 (1995)

Thorne, Barrie, Kramarae, Cheris and Henley, Nancy (eds.), *Language, Gender and Society*, Heinle & Heinle, Boston (1983)

Tucker, Nita, *How NOT to Stay Single*, Crown Publishers (1996)

Tyler, C. W., 'Cyclopean vision', in Regan, D. (ed.), 'Vision and visual dysfunction', *Binocular Vision*, Vol. 9, Macmillan, New York (1989)

Von Cranach, M., *Social Communication and Movement: Studies of Interaction and Expression in Man and Chimpanzee*, Academic Press, London (1973)

Vrij, A., *Detecting Lies and Deceit*, John Wiley (2001)

Vrij, A, Vrij, G. R. and Bull, R., 'Insight into behavior displayed during deception', *Human Communication Research*, 22 (4), 544–62 (1996)

Vrij, 'Credibility judgments of detectives: the impact of nonverbal behavior, social skills, and physical characteristics on impression formation', *The Journal of Social Psychology*, 133, 601–10 (1993)

Wainwright, G. R., *Teach Yourself Body Language*, Hodder & Stoughton (1985)

Wegesin, D. J., 'Relation between language lateralisation and spatial ability in gay and straight women and men', *Laterality*, 3, 227–39 (1998)

Weisfeld, G. E. and Beresford, J. M., 'Erectness of posture as an indicator of dominance or success in humans', *Motivation and Emotion*, Vol. 6 (2)

Weisfeld and Linkey, H. E., 'Dominance displays as indicators of social success motive', *Motivation and Emotion*

Westheimer, Ruth, *Dr Ruth's Guide to Good Sex*, Warner, New York (1986)

White, A. G., 'The patient sits down: a clinical note', *Psychosomatic Medicine* (1953)

Whiteside, R. L., *Face Language II*, Frederick Fell, Hollywood, FL (1988)

Whiteside, *Face Language*, Pocket Books, New York (1975)

Whitney, Hubin and Murphy, *The New Psychology of Persuasion and Motivation in Selling*, Prentice-Hall, New Jersey (1978)

Wilson, Edward O., *Sociobiology: The New Synthesis*, Harvard University Press, Cambridge (1975)

Wilson, Glenn D. and Nias, David, *The Mystery of Love*, Open Books, London (1976)

Wilson, P. R., 'Perceptual distortion of height as a function of ascribed academic status', *Journal of Social Psychology* (1968)

Winston Macauley, Marnie, *Manspeak*, Newport House (1996)

Witleson, S. F., 'The brain connection: the corpus collosum is larger in left-handers', *Science* 229, 665–8 (1985)

Witleson, 'Sex differences in the neurology of cognition: psychological, social, educational and clinical implications', in Sullerot, E. (ed.), *Le Fait Féminin*, Fayard, Paris, 287–303 (1978)

Witleson, 'Sex and the single hemisphere: specialisation of the right hemisphere for spatial processing', *Science*, 193, 425–7 (1976)

Witleson, 'Hemispheric specialisation for linguistic and non-linguistic tactual perception using a dichotomous stimulation technique', *Cortex*, 10, 3–7 (1974)

Witleson, 'Left hemisphere specialisation for language in the newborn brain', *Science*, 96, 641–6 (1973)

Wolf, Naomi, *The Beauty Myth*, Anchor, New York (1992)

Wolfe, C., *A Psychology of Gesture*, Methuen, London (1948)

Wright, Robert, *The Moral Animal*, Pantheon, New York (1994)

Young, J. Z., *An Introduction to the Study of Man*, Oxford University Press, New York (1971)

Zappia, J. V. and Rogers, L. J., 'Sex differences and the reversal of brain asymmetry by testosterone in chickens', *Behavioural Brain Research*, 23, 261–7 (1987)

Why not use Allan Pease as guest speaker for your next conference or seminar?

Pease International (Australia) Pty Ltd
Pease International (UK) Ltd

P.O. Box 1260
Buderim 4556
Queensland
AUSTRALIA
Tel: ++61 7 5445 5600
Fax: ++61 7 5445 5688

Liberty House
16 Newbold Terrace
Leamington Spa CV32 4EG
UNITED KINGDOM
Tel: ++44 (0) 1926 889900
Fax: ++44 (0) 1926 421100

email: (Aust) info@peaseinternational.com
          (UK) ukoffice@peaseinternational.com
website: www.peaseinternational.com

Also by Allan Pease:

Video Programs
Body Language Series
Silent Signals
The Interview
How to Make Appointments by Telephone

DVD Programs
The Best of Body Language
How to Develop Powerful Communication—Managing the
    Differences Between Men and Women

Audio Programs
The Four Personality Styles
How to Make Appointments by Telephone
How to Remember Names, Faces & Lists
Why Men Don't Listen and Women Can't Read Maps
Questions are the Answers

Books
The Definitive Book of Body Language
Why Men Don't Listen & Women Can't Read Maps
Why Men Lie and Women Cry
Why Men Can Only Do One Thing At A Time & Women Never
    Stop Talking
How Compatible Are You?
Talk Language
Write Language
Questions are the Answers
The Bumper Book of Rude & Politically Incorrect Jokes
Politically Incorrect Jokes Men Love